BUDGETING FOR BEGINNERS

A Smart Money Roadmap
to Financial Freedom

BRIAN COLLINS

Copyright © 2025 Brian Collins
All rights reserved.

No part of this publication may be copied, stored, or shared—by any method, whether electronic, mechanical, photocopied, recorded, or otherwise—without prior written permission from Enlighten Publications.

Some uses may fall under fair use or fair dealing laws in certain countries, such as for research, private study, criticism, or review. For all other uses, including reproduction, distribution, or licensing, please contact the Rights Department at Enlighten Publications.

Trademarks
All trademarks and brand names mentioned in this book are acknowledged. The publisher makes no claim to proprietary rights in them.

Credits
Cover design: Sophie Russell
Editing: Harper Lang Editorial
Interior design and typesetting: Typographica

Disclaimer
This book is for educational and informational purposes only. It does not constitute legal, medical, financial, or other professional advice. The author and publisher accept no responsibility for any errors, omissions, or consequences arising from the use of this material. Readers should consult qualified professionals before making decisions based on the content of this book.

ISBN
978-1-916720-33-6

BEFORE WE BEGIN

This is not just a book. It is a beginning.

A deliberate step forward - the moment you chose to take your financial story into your own hands.

Money may have lived in your mind as a riddle unsolved. Perhaps a weight that pressed against your thoughts, a fog that obscured clarity, or a subject left unspoken. But now, you're turning toward understanding, steadiness, and agency.

Perfect isn't the requirement. Wealth isn't the prerequisite. Starting is.

Each chapter will help you unwind inherited beliefs and replace them with direction. Each tool will reshape your daily choices with awareness. And with steady practice, you will construct something vital: a financial foundation built on what matters to you, not what frightens you.

This isn't about mere survival. This is about creating possibility.

Take a moment. Then move forward.

You've already taken the hardest step.

Welcome.

TABLE OF CONTENTS

Introduction 1

    Unlock Your Financial Potential 1

The Budgeting Mindset, Why Budgeting Is Your New Superpower 3

    Debunking Common Budget Myths 4

    Identifying Your 'Money Story' 6

    The Power of Purposeful Spending 8

    Your Financial Mindset Shift 10

Know Your Numbers, Income, Expenses, and Hidden Costs 13

    Mapping Your Money Inflow 15

    Confronting the Expense List 17

    Spotting Hidden Financial Pitfalls 20

    Your Money Map: Know Where You Stand 22

Designing Your Dream Budget, Step by Step 25

    Setting Up Your Categories 27

    The 50/30/20 Rule and Variations 30

    Bring On the Worksheets! 33

    Your Blueprint for Financial Success 35

Setting Goals That Stick, Short-Term and Long-Term 39

    Creating SMART Financial Goals 41

    Visualizing Success 44

    Balancing Short-Term Wins and Long-Term Vision 47

    Dream It, Plan It, Achieve It 51

Saving Secrets, The Art of Building Your Safety Net 53

    Emergency Fund Essentials 56

    Automating Your Savings 57

    Best Practices for Consistent Growth 59

    Your Savings Superpower 61

Taming the Debt Beast, Strategies to Reduce and Eliminate 63

    Understanding 'Good Debt' vs. 'Bad Debt' 65

    Snowball vs. Avalanche Methods 68

Staying Motivated Through the Payoff Journey 70
Debt-Free and Thriving 73

Living Frugally Without Feeling Deprived 77

Frugal Hacks You Can Start Today 79
Meal Planning and Lifestyle Tweaks............................. 81
Mindset Shifts for Sustainable Saving 84
Smart Spending, Happy Living...................................... 86

Beginner-Friendly Investment Pathways 89

Low-Risk Savings and CDs 91
Index Funds 101 92
When and How to Level Up Your Investments........................... 94
Planting Seeds for Future Wealth................................... 97

Tracking, Reviewing, and Adjusting Your Budget 101

Review Cycles and Check-Ins 103
Embracing Flexibility 105
Real-Life Examples and Success Stories.................................. 107
Fine-Tuning Your Financial Plan 110

Staying the Course, Your Roadmap to Financial Freedom........ 113

Overcoming Plateaus and Setbacks......................... 115
Continual Learning and Financial Growth 117
Celebrating Milestones and Looking Ahead 120
Your Journey to Financial Freedom Continues....................... 121

INTRODUCTION

UNLOCK YOUR FINANCIAL POTENTIAL

Welcome to *Budgeting for Beginners: A Smart Money Roadmap to Financial Freedom*. If you're picking up this book, it means you're ready to take a profound and exciting step toward understanding and mastering your finances. Congratulations on making this life-changing decision!

I'm Brian Collins, and I understand firsthand how daunting the world of personal finance can feel. Like many people, I used to think that budgeting was a complex, restrictive chore---something that required advanced math skills and hours of tedious paperwork. But as I began to educate myself and put simple strategies into practice, I realized that effective budgeting is actually an empowering tool, one that can help anyone achieve their financial dreams.

Throughout this book, my goal is to be your trusted guide and mentor, demystifying the key principles of budgeting in a way that feels accessible, engaging, and even enjoyable. We'll start by exploring the fundamental building blocks of personal finance, such as understanding the difference between income and expenses, identifying your unique spending habits and money beliefs, and embracing the transformative power of purposeful spending.

From there, we'll dive into the step-by-step process of crafting a budget that truly works for you. You'll learn how to track your cash flow, categorize your expenses, and use proven frameworks like the 50/30/20 rule to create a spending plan that aligns with your values and goals. But more than just teaching you the mechanics of budgeting, this book aims to help you cultivate a positive, growth-oriented mindset around money. We'll explore strategies for setting and achieving both short-term and long-term financial goals, building a robust emergency fund, and making frugality a satisfying part of your lifestyle.

As we journey together through these pages, you'll also gain a deeper understanding of how to tackle common financial challenges, such as managing debt, navigating changes in income or expenses, and making informed decisions about basic investments. With each chapter, you'll develop greater confidence and clarity around your finances, empowering you to take control of your money story once and for all.

At its core, budgeting is about so much more than numbers on a spreadsheet. It's about creating a life of abundance, security, and financial freedom. It's about aligning your spending with your deepest values and aspirations, and building a strong foundation for your future. With the tools, insights, and real-life examples in this book, you'll be well-equipped to do just that.

So, dear reader, are you ready to embark on this transformative journey? To unlock your full financial potential and create a budget that truly serves your life? If so, I invite you to dive in with an open mind and a willing heart. Your path to financial freedom starts right here, right now.

Let's get started!

CHAPTER ONE

THE BUDGETING MINDSET, WHY BUDGETING IS YOUR NEW SUPERPOWER

Welcome to your journey towards financial freedom! In this chapter, we'll explore the transformative power of adopting a budgeting mindset. If you're like most people, the mere mention of the word "budget" might conjure up feelings of restriction, deprivation, or even dread. But what if I told you that budgeting is actually the key to unlocking a life of abundance, purpose, and joy?

At its core, a budget is simply a plan for how you will allocate your income to meet your needs, wants, and financial goals. It's not about cutting out all the fun and spontaneity from your life, but rather about being intentional with your spending so you can enjoy the things that truly matter to you. When you approach budgeting with the right mindset, it becomes a powerful tool for aligning your money with your values and creating the life you desire.

Throughout this chapter, we'll debunk some of the most common myths and misconceptions about budgeting that keep people stuck in a cycle of financial stress and unfulfillment. We'll explore how our personal money stories - the beliefs and experiences that shape our attitudes towards money - can either hold us back or propel us forward on our financial journey. And we'll dive into the concept of purposeful spending, learning how to make financial choices that honor our deepest values and priorities.

By the end of this chapter, you'll have a newfound appreciation for the role that budgeting can play in your life. You'll see that it's not about deprivation or restriction, but rather about empowerment and abundance. You'll have the tools and mindset you need to start creating a budget that works for you - one that supports your dreams, aligns with your values, and helps you build the financial future you deserve.

So let's dive in and discover why budgeting truly is your new superpower on the path to financial freedom. In the first section, we'll start by debunking some of the most persistent myths about budgeting that may be holding you back from embracing this powerful tool.

Debunking Common Budget Myths

When it comes to managing our finances, we've all heard our fair share of budgeting advice—some helpful, some not so much. Unfortunately, there are quite a few persistent myths about budgeting that can hold us back from achieving the financial security and freedom we desire. Let's take a closer look at these misconceptions, understand where they come from, and see how we can move past them to create a healthier relationship with our money.

One of the most common myths is that budgeting is all about restriction and deprivation. We often imagine that living on a budget means saying goodbye to dining out, travel, and all the little luxuries that make life enjoyable. This belief usually stems from a misunderstanding of what a budget actually is. At its core, a budget is simply a plan for how you will allocate your income to meet your needs, wants, and financial goals. It's not about cutting out all the fun, but rather about being intentional with your spending so you can enjoy life while also staying on track financially.

Think of it this way: if you were planning a road trip, you wouldn't just hop in the car and start driving without a map or a destination in mind. You'd likely plan out your route, estimate your expenses for gas, food, and lodging, and make sure you have enough money saved up to cover the costs. Budgeting is a lot like that. It's about having a clear picture of where your money is going and making informed decisions about how to allocate it based on your priorities and goals.

Another myth that often holds people back is the idea that you need to be a math whiz or financial expert to create and stick to a budget. In reality, budgeting is a skill that anyone can learn with a bit of practice and the right tools. You don't need a degree in accounting to track your income and expenses, set financial goals, and make a plan to reach them. There are plenty of simple, user-friendly budgeting apps and templates available that can help you get started, even if numbers aren't your strong suit.

For example, imagine you're a busy working parent who feels like there's never enough time or mental energy to sit down and crunch numbers. You might feel intimidated by the idea of creating a budget from scratch, but you could start by using a budgeting app that connects to your bank account and automatically categorizes your transactions. This can give you a clear picture of where your money is going without requiring hours of manual tracking. From there, you can set up simple budget categories and spending limits based on your income and goals, and the app can help you stay accountable with regular check-ins and progress reports.

A third common myth is that budgeting is only for people who are struggling financially or living paycheck to paycheck. In truth, budgeting is a valuable tool for anyone who wants to be proactive about their financial health, regardless of their income level or current financial situation. Whether you're just starting out in your career, raising a family, or nearing retirement, having a clear plan for your money can help you make the most of your resources and achieve your short-term and long-term goals.

Consider the example of a young professional who landed a high-paying job right out of college. With a hefty paycheck hitting their bank account each month, they might feel like they don't need to budget or watch their spending too closely. However, without a plan in place, it's all too easy to fall into the trap of lifestyle inflation, where your spending habits gradually creep up to match your income. By creating a budget early on, this young professional could ensure they're saving enough for the future, investing wisely, and making room for the things that matter most to them, like travel or starting a business.

As we can see, budgeting is not about restriction, deprivation, or financial expertise. It's about empowering yourself to take control of your money and use it in a way that aligns with your values and goals. By debunking these common myths and reframing the way we think about budgeting, we can start to see it as a powerful tool for creating the life we want, both now and in the future.

So, now that we've cleared up some of these misconceptions, let's dive a bit deeper into our personal money stories and how they shape our financial habits and attitudes. By examining our unique beliefs and experiences around money, we can start to build a budgeting mindset that works for us.

IDENTIFYING YOUR 'MONEY STORY'

Our attitudes and behaviors around money are deeply influenced by our personal beliefs and experiences, often in ways we may not even realize. Every one of us has a unique "money story"—a narrative shaped by our upbringing, family dynamics, cultural background, and life events. These stories can have a powerful impact on how we approach financial decisions, from everyday spending habits to long-term investing strategies.

For some of us, our money stories may be rooted in scarcity and fear. Perhaps we grew up in a household where money was always tight, and we internalized the belief that there's never enough to go around. This experience can lead to a range of behaviors in adulthood, such as compulsive saving, fear of investing, or even self-sabotaging spending habits. On the other hand, some of us may have grown up with a sense of abundance and security around money. We might have been taught that money is a tool for enjoying life and helping others, leading us to approach financial decisions with confidence and optimism.

Our money stories can also be shaped by the messages we absorb from society and the media. From a young age, we're bombarded with images and ideas about what it means to be successful, happy, and financially secure. We might internalize the belief that we need to keep up with the Joneses, chasing after the latest gadgets, fashion trends, or lifestyle markers of success. Or we might absorb the idea that money is the root of all evil, leading us to feel guilt or shame around our financial desires and choices.

Whatever our individual money stories may be, the first step to creating a healthier relationship with money is to bring these stories into conscious awareness. By examining our beliefs and experiences around money, we can start to untangle the ways in which they may be holding us back or shaping our financial habits in unproductive ways.

Here's a short reflective exercise to help you start uncovering your own money story:

1. Take a few moments to think back on your earliest memories around money. What messages did you absorb from your family, friends, or community about what money meant and how it should be used? Write down a few key beliefs or phrases that stand out.

2. Consider a recent financial decision you made — whether it was a major purchase, an investment choice, or a budgeting decision. What emotions or thoughts came up for you as you were making this decision? Did you feel confident and empowered, or anxious and uncertain? Try to trace these feelings back to specific experiences or beliefs from your past.

3. Imagine your ideal relationship with money. What would it look like to feel truly at peace and in control of your finances? What beliefs or attitudes would you need to cultivate to get there? Write down a few key phrases or affirmations that embody this vision.

As you go through this exercise, remember to approach your money story with curiosity and compassion. Our financial beliefs and habits are often deeply ingrained, and it can take time and patience to shift them. The goal is not to judge or blame ourselves for past choices, but rather to bring greater awareness and intentionality to our relationship with money moving forward.

One helpful way to reframe our money stories is to focus on the idea of financial empowerment. Rather than seeing money as a source of stress or scarcity, we can choose to view it as a tool for creating the life we want. By taking control of our financial choices and aligning our spending with our values, we can start to write a new chapter in our money story—one that is characterized by abundance, freedom, and purposeful living.

As we continue on this journey of financial self-discovery, let's explore the concept of purposeful spending in more depth. By learning to make financial choices that align with our deepest values and priorities, we can transform our relationship with money from one of deprivation and guilt to one of empowerment and joy.

THE POWER OF PURPOSEFUL SPENDING

At the heart of every successful budget is a clear understanding of what truly matters to you—your deepest values, goals, and priorities. When we align our spending habits with these core principles, we tap into a profound sense of purpose and fulfillment that goes far beyond the fleeting pleasure of impulse purchases. This is the power of purposeful spending.

Too often, we fall into the trap of letting our spending habits dictate our lives, rather than the other way around. We see something we want in the moment—a shiny new gadget, a trendy outfit, or a lavish night out—and we act on that impulse without stopping to consider whether it aligns with our larger financial goals or personal values. Over time, these small, unconscious choices can add up to a life that feels out of sync with our deepest desires and aspirations.

The key to breaking free from this cycle of unfulfilling spending is to cultivate a mindset of intentionality and purpose. This means taking the time to get clear on what really matters to you—not just in terms of your financial goals, but in terms of your overall life vision. What kind of experiences, relationships, and accomplishments do you want to prioritize? What legacy do you want to leave behind? By answering these bigger questions, you can start to create a roadmap for your spending that is grounded in your authentic self.

For example, let's say one of your core values is adventure and exploration. You might prioritize saving up for a once-in-a-lifetime travel experience, even if it means cutting back on daily luxuries like eating out or subscribing to streaming services. Or perhaps you're passionate about lifelong learning and personal growth. In that case, you might choose to invest in courses, workshops, or coaching programs that help you develop new skills and expand your horizons.

The beauty of purposeful spending is that it shifts the focus from deprivation to abundance. Rather than feeling like you're constantly saying "no" to the things you want, you're saying a resounding "yes" to the things that truly enrich and fulfill you. You're not just cutting back for the sake of saving money, but rather making a conscious choice to direct your resources toward the people, experiences, and causes that matter most.

Of course, making this shift from impulse spending to purposeful spending is easier said than done. Our consumer culture is designed to prey on our desires and insecurities, bombarding us with messages that we need to buy more, have more, and be more in order to be happy and successful. It takes real mindfulness and discipline to resist these temptations and stay true to our larger goals.

One helpful practice is to create a "spending pause" before making any significant purchase. Rather than acting on an impulse in the moment, give yourself a set period of time—whether it's a few hours, a few days, or even a few weeks—to reflect on whether the purchase aligns with your values and priorities. Ask yourself questions like: "Will this purchase bring me lasting joy and fulfillment, or just a temporary high? Is there something else I'd rather be saving toward? How will I feel about this purchase a month or a year from now?"

Another useful strategy is to create visual reminders of your larger financial goals and priorities. This might be a vision board that showcases images of your dream home, your ideal retirement lifestyle, or the places you want to travel. Or it might be a simple list of your core values and the specific financial milestones you want to achieve. By keeping these visual cues front and center, you can train your brain to focus on the bigger picture rather than getting caught up in the momentary desires.

Ultimately, the power of purposeful spending lies in its ability to transform our relationship with money from one of scarcity and deprivation to one of abundance and joy. When we let our deepest values and aspirations guide our financial choices, we free ourselves from the endless cycle of wanting more and never feeling satisfied. We learn to find contentment and fulfillment in the present moment, even as we work toward our larger goals and dreams.

As we continue on this journey of aligning our money with our purpose, let's take a closer look at the nuts and bolts of creating a values-driven budget. In the next section, we'll explore how to map out your income and expenses in a way that supports your authentic priorities and paves the way for lasting financial freedom.

YOUR FINANCIAL MINDSET SHIFT

In the first chapter, we dove deep into the transformative power of adopting a budgeting mindset. We explored how shifting your perspective on money management can open up a world of possibility, freedom, and fulfillment. Let's take a moment to reflect on the key insights and lessons we've learned so far.

First and foremost, we discovered that budgeting is not about restriction or deprivation, but rather about aligning your spending with your values and goals. By debunking common myths and misconceptions, we saw how a budget can be a tool for empowerment, not punishment. When you approach money management with intention and purpose, you gain clarity and control over your financial life.

We also explored the concept of our personal "money stories" — the beliefs and experiences that shape our attitudes and behaviors around finances. By examining these often subconscious narratives, we can start to untangle

Budgeting for Beginners

unhelpful patterns and rewrite our money stories from a place of abundance and possibility. This self-awareness is a crucial first step in crafting a healthy, joyful relationship with money.

Another key insight from Chapter One was the power of purposeful spending. By focusing our resources on the things that truly matter to us — the experiences, relationships, and goals that light us up inside — we can find deep satisfaction and meaning, even with a limited budget. Aligning our money with our values is the secret to financial peace and contentment.

As we let these lessons sink in, it's important to remember that adopting a budgeting mindset is a journey, not a destination. Like any new skill or habit, it takes practice, patience, and self-compassion to fully integrate these principles into your life. But with each small shift in perspective, each intentional choice, you'll be building the foundation for lasting financial well-being.

So take a moment to celebrate how far you've already come. Honor the courage and curiosity that brought you to this book, and the commitment you've shown in absorbing these early lessons. Your openness to growth and change is already setting you apart from the crowd.

And now, with a solid understanding of the budgeting mindset under your belt, you're ready to dive into the nuts and bolts of money management. In the next chapter, we'll explore the key building blocks of any successful budget: income, expenses, and savings. By gaining a clear, honest picture of your financial landscape, you'll be well on your way to crafting a spending plan that supports your dreams and values.

So turn the page with excitement and anticipation, knowing that each new insight and skill is bringing you closer to the financial life you desire. Your journey to abundance, peace, and purpose is just beginning — and the best is yet to come.

CHAPTER TWO

KNOW YOUR NUMBERS, INCOME, EXPENSES, AND HIDDEN COSTS

Welcome to the nitty-gritty of budgeting! In this chapter, we're going to dive into the foundation of any solid financial plan: knowing your numbers. Just like a GPS needs accurate starting and ending points to map out the best route, creating a budget that truly works for you requires a clear and comprehensive understanding of your financial inflows and outflows.

We'll start by taking a detailed look at your income. This might seem straightforward at first glance—just the number on your paycheck, right? But as we'll explore, there are often many sources of money flowing into your life beyond your primary job. From side hustles and freelance gigs to investment dividends and birthday checks from Grandma, we'll learn how to map out a complete picture of your revenue streams. Like a detective piecing together clues, we'll gather all the data points that make up your unique financial landscape.

But of course, a budget isn't just about what's coming in; it's also about where that money is going. That's why the next step in our journey will be confronting the expense list. We'll learn how to categorize and track your spending, distinguishing between non-negotiable costs like housing and more flexible areas like entertainment. We'll explore strategies for combing through your bank statements with an eagle eye, spotting patterns and opportunities for savings. Think of it like a treasure hunt, but instead of seeking gold, you're looking for coins in the proverbial couch cushions of your spending habits!

As we dig deeper into the expense side of the equation, we'll also learn how to spot those sneaky financial pitfalls that can derail even the best-laid budget plans. From subscription services that siphon away cash each month to the slow leak of daily latte habits, we'll shine a light on the hidden costs that can add up over time. By developing a keen awareness of these money traps, you'll be better equipped to dodge them and keep your budget on track.

Now, confronting the raw numbers of your financial life can feel a bit overwhelming at first. It's easy to slip into judgment or shame, especially if you're not quite where you want to be. But remember, this process is not about dwelling on past missteps or beating yourself up over every dollar spent. Instead, it's about empowering yourself with clear, objective data so that you can make informed choices moving forward. Think of it like stepping on the scale before starting a fitness journey; the number itself is neutral—it's simply a starting point from which to chart your progress.

Throughout this chapter, we'll be focusing on two key themes. The first is completeness. Like a scientist gathering data for an experiment, we want to capture all the relevant information about your financial life, not just the obvious bits. The more comprehensive your income and expense portrait is, the easier it will be to create a budget that fits like a well-tailored suit.

The second theme is awareness. By shining a bright light on your numbers, you're taking the first crucial step towards financial empowerment. It's like the old adage says: "What gets measured gets managed." Simply by paying attention to your money flows, you're already shifting your relationship with your finances from passive to proactive.

So take a deep breath, grab your favorite beverage and a notepad, and let's dive in! In the next section, we'll start by mapping out all the ways money flows into your life. Think of it as a treasure map leading towards your financial goals—and we're going to make sure no coin gets left behind.

Mapping Your Money Inflow

To create a budget that truly works for you, the first step is to get a clear and comprehensive picture of your income. This means looking beyond just your regular paycheck and identifying all the ways that money flows into your life. By taking a thorough, systematic approach to mapping your money inflow, you can gain a more empowered and proactive stance toward your finances.

Let's start with the most obvious source of income for most people: your primary job. If you're employed full-time or part-time, this is likely where the bulk of your money comes from. Be sure to use your net income (the amount that actually hits your bank account after taxes and other deductions) rather than your gross pay. This will give you a more accurate sense of how much you have to work with each month.

But what about other sources of income? Many of us have money coming in from places beyond our main gig. For example:

- Do you have any side hustles or freelance work that brings in extra cash? This might include things like driving for a ride-share service, selling handmade crafts online, or picking up occasional shifts at a local business.

- Do you receive any money from rental properties or investments, such as stocks, bonds, or real estate?

- Are there any other regular payments you receive, such as child support, alimony, or a pension?

- Do you ever get cash gifts for birthdays or holidays that you could factor into your budget?

The key is to cast a wide net and think creatively about all the ways money comes into your world. Even small amounts can add up over time, so it's worth taking a comprehensive view.

One helpful way to organize this information is to create a simple income tracking worksheet. This can be done with pen and paper, a spreadsheet program like Excel, or even a note-taking app on your phone. The format can be as basic or detailed as you like.

As you fill in your own income sources and amounts, a few tips to keep in mind:

1. Be as specific as possible. The more detailed and accurate your income picture is, the easier it will be to create a realistic, workable budget. Don't worry about getting it perfect right away – you can always adjust and refine as you go along.

2. Use averages for irregular income. If you have income sources that fluctuate from month to month (like freelance work or side gigs), try to come up with a monthly average based on your earnings over the past

few months or year. This can help smooth out the ups and downs and give you a more stable baseline to work with.

3. Don't forget annual or one-time payments. Things like tax refunds, performance bonuses, or even garage sale proceeds may not come every month, but they're still part of your overall financial picture. You can choose to factor these in as part of your regular monthly budget (by dividing the total by 12) or earmark them for specific goals and priorities.

4. Consider your household, not just yourself. If you share finances with a partner, spouse, or family members, be sure to include their income sources as well for a complete picture. This can also be a great opportunity to get on the same page about your shared financial goals and values.

Once you've mapped out all your sources of income, take a moment to reflect on what this information tells you. Are there any areas where you'd like to see your income grow? Are there any revenue streams you might be overlooking or underutilizing? Simply having a clear, big-picture view of your money inflow can spark new insights and ideas for optimizing your earning potential.

Armed with this foundational knowledge about your income, you'll be well-positioned to tackle the next key piece of the budgeting puzzle: gaining a clear-eyed view of your expenses. Let's dive into that crucial step in the next section.

CONFRONTING THE EXPENSE LIST

Now that we've got a handle on your income, it's time to take a clear-eyed look at where that money is going each month. This can be one of the most challenging parts of the budgeting process, as it requires us to confront our spending habits head-on and make some tough choices about what to prioritize. But by breaking down your expenses into manageable categories and looking for opportunities to trim the fat, you can take control of your financial outflow and free up more resources for the things that matter most.

Let's start by understanding the two main types of expenses: fixed and variable. Fixed expenses are those bills that stay relatively constant from month to month, such as:

- Rent or mortgage payments

- Car payments

- Insurance premiums (health, car, home, etc.)

- Student loan payments

- Phone and internet bills

- Gym memberships or subscription services

These expenses are often non-negotiable in the short term, meaning you're committed to paying them each month regardless of your other financial priorities. That's why it's so important to keep these costs as lean as possible, shopping around for the best rates and only committing to ongoing bills that truly justify their value in your life.

Variable expenses, on the other hand, are those costs that fluctuate from month to month based on your consumption and behavior. These might include:

- Groceries and dining out

- Utilities like electricity, gas, and water (which can vary seasonally)

- Transportation costs like gas, parking, and public transit

- Entertainment and leisure activities

- Clothing and personal care items

- Home maintenance and repairs

- Pet care and supplies

- Travel and gifts

These expenses tend to be more flexible and discretionary, meaning you have greater control over how much you spend in each category. This is often where the greatest opportunities for savings and optimization lie.

To get a clear picture of your monthly expense breakdown, it can be helpful to comb through your bank and credit card statements from the past few months and categorize each transaction into its appropriate bucket. You may be surprised at how quickly certain costs add up, like daily coffee runs or impulse purchases at the checkout counter.

As you review your expenses, keep an eye out for any recurring charges that may have slipped through the cracks, like subscriptions you no longer use or memberships you forgot to cancel. These "zombie expenses" can bleed your budget dry without providing any real value in return. Don't be afraid to pick up the phone and negotiate with service providers for better rates or promotional deals, especially for things like cable, internet, or insurance. A few minutes of haggling can often yield significant savings over the course of a year.

Another helpful strategy is to look for patterns in your variable expenses that may signal opportunities for behavior change. For example, if you notice that a large chunk of your food budget is going toward takeout and restaurant meals, you might challenge yourself to cook more at home or prep meals in advance to save money and improve your health. Or if your utility bills are consistently high, you could make a game out of finding creative ways to conserve energy and water each month, like taking shorter showers or adjusting your thermostat a few degrees.

As you work through your expense categories, remember that the goal is not necessarily to cut every cost to the bone, but rather to align your spending with your values and priorities. Some expenses, like investing in your education or supporting causes you believe in, may be worth the extra outlay because they contribute to your long-term growth and fulfillment. The key is to be intentional about where you choose to direct your hard-earned dollars, rather than letting your spending habits run on autopilot.

Of course, even the most diligent expense tracking and budgeting can be derailed by unexpected costs and financial curveballs. That's why it's so important to build a buffer into your budget for life's little (and not-so-little) surprises. In the next section, we'll explore some strategies for spotting these hidden money traps and building resilience into your financial plan. By staying alert to the ways that small expenses can add up over time, you can keep your budget on track and your financial goals within reach.

Spotting Hidden Financial Pitfalls

One of the sneakiest ways our budgets can get derailed is through small, recurring expenses that fly under the radar of our conscious awareness. These hidden financial pitfalls come in many forms—subscription services we signed up for and forgot about, convenience fees tacked onto our regular purchases, or even just the steady drip of our daily coffee habit. While these costs might seem insignificant in the moment, they have a pesky way of adding up over time and eating away at our financial progress.

Let's take the example of subscription services. In our modern age of digital convenience, it's easier than ever to sign up for a streaming platform, gaming service, or premium app with just the click of a button. Many of these subscriptions start with an enticing free trial period or promotional rate, making them feel like a no-brainer in the short term. But fast forward a few months (or even years), and you might find yourself saddled with a dozen or more recurring charges that you barely remember signing up for, let alone use on a regular basis.

Imagine you signed up for a premium music streaming service at a discounted rate of $4.99 per month. At first, that $5 charge barely registers as a blip on your financial radar—it's the equivalent of a fancy coffee drink or a quick fast food meal. But if you let that subscription linger unnoticed for a year, you've suddenly spent nearly $60 on a service you may not be fully utilizing. Now multiply that by a handful of other forgotten subscriptions—a fitness app here, a premium storage service there—and you can easily see how these small expenses start to snowball.

The same principle applies to convenience fees, those sneaky surcharges that get tacked onto everything from concert tickets to food delivery orders. While paying an extra $2 or $3 in the moment might not feel like a dealbreaker, these fees can quickly add up if they become a regular part of your spending habits.

If you order takeout with a $3 delivery fee just twice a week, for example, you're looking at an extra $312 per year in fees alone—not to mention the marked-up cost of the food itself compared to cooking at home.

Even our most mundane daily habits can take a toll on our budgets over time. Take the classic example of a daily coffee shop habit. Let's say you stop by your favorite café on your way to work each morning and treat yourself to a $4 latte. In the grand scheme of your overall budget, $4 might feel like a trivial expense—a small luxury that helps you start your day on a positive note. But do the math over the course of a year, and that daily latte habit is costing you over $1,000 annually. That's a significant chunk of change that could be redirected toward paying off debt, saving for a big purchase, or investing in your future.

So how can we avoid falling prey to these hidden budget traps? The key is to make a habit of regularly reviewing your expenses with a fine-toothed comb. Set aside some time each month (or at least each quarter) to comb through your bank and credit card statements, looking for any recurring charges or subtle spending patterns that might be flying under the radar.

As you review, ask yourself:

- Am I actually using this subscription or service regularly?

- Is this expense bringing me real value or joy, or has it become more of a mindless habit?

- Are there any areas where I'm consistently spending more than I realized, like takeout meals or impulse purchases?

- Could I find a cheaper alternative or substitute for this expense that would be just as satisfying?

Remember, the goal isn't necessarily to eliminate every small luxury or convenience from your life in the name of saving money. Rather, it's about being intentional and clear-eyed about where your money is going, and making sure that your spending habits are aligned with your bigger-picture financial goals and values. By staying vigilant to the hidden costs that can derail your budget over time, you can free up more resources for the things that truly matter to you.

Of course, knowing where your money is going is just the first step in the budgeting process. The next challenge is to take that knowledge and use it to craft a spending plan that helps you make the most of your hard-earned cash. In the next section, we'll dive into the nuts and bolts of designing your ideal budget—one that balances your short-term needs with your long-term financial dreams. With a clear roadmap in place, you'll be well on your way to turning your money into a powerful tool for crafting the life you want.

YOUR MONEY MAP: KNOW WHERE YOU STAND

In Chapter Two, we embarked on a journey of financial self-discovery, diving into the critical components of our money landscape: income, expenses, and hidden costs. By shining a light on these key areas, we laid the groundwork for crafting a budget that is both realistic and empowering. Let's take a moment to review the essential insights and lessons from this chapter.

First, we learned the importance of mapping out our money inflow. This means taking a comprehensive look at all the ways money comes into our lives, from regular paychecks to side hustle earnings to investment dividends. By understanding the full scope of our income, we gain a clearer picture of our financial resources and potential.

Next, we confronted the expense side of the equation. We explored how to categorize our spending into fixed and variable expenses, and how to comb through our bills and statements with an eagle eye. This process helps us identify areas where we might be overspending, as well as opportunities to trim costs and redirect funds toward our goals.

A key insight from this chapter was the concept of hidden financial pitfalls. We discovered how small, recurring expenses like subscriptions, convenience fees, and daily habits can add up over time, quietly eroding our budget. By bringing awareness to these sneaky money traps, we can make more intentional choices and keep our spending in alignment with our values.

Throughout this process of financial self-discovery, we emphasized the importance of maintaining a curious, compassionate attitude. Confronting the raw numbers of our money life can stir up a range of emotions, from shame to anxiety to overwhelm. By approaching this exploration with a spirit of non-judgment and openness, we create space for honest reflection and growth.

As we absorb these lessons, it's crucial to remember that knowledge is power. Simply by gaining a clear understanding of your income, expenses, and hidden costs, you're already taking a giant step toward financial empowerment. You're equipping yourself with the information and awareness needed to make thoughtful, proactive choices about your money.

So take a moment to celebrate this newfound clarity and insight. Honor the courage it takes to shine a light on your financial landscape, and the wisdom you've gained in the process. With this foundation of self-knowledge, you're now ready to start crafting a budget that truly serves your life and goals.

In the next chapter, we'll explore how to transform this raw financial data into a flexible, dynamic spending plan. You'll learn proven strategies for allocating your resources, balancing competing priorities, and adjusting your budget as life evolves. With your money map as a guide, you'll be well on your way to charting a course toward financial freedom and fulfillment.

So embrace this journey of self-discovery, and trust in the power of awareness to transform your relationship with money. The more you understand your financial landscape, the more equipped you'll be to cultivate a life of intention, purpose, and abundance. Onward!

CHAPTER THREE

DESIGNING YOUR DREAM BUDGET, STEP BY STEP

Let's dive into the exciting world of budget design! In this chapter, we'll explore how to craft a spending plan that not only covers your basic needs but also supports your biggest dreams and aspirations. Think of it like building a dream home for your finances—a place where every dollar has a purpose and every expense is aligned with your values and goals.

We'll start by walking through the process of setting up your budget categories. Just like an architect carefully considers each room in a house, we'll think through the different spending areas that make up your financial life. From the essential "load-bearing walls" of housing, food, and healthcare to the "decorative flourishes" of hobbies, travel, and giving, we'll make sure your budget reflects your unique lifestyle and priorities.

But how do you know how much to allocate to each category? That's where the 50/30/20 rule comes in. This simple but powerful framework suggests dividing your after-tax income into three main buckets: 50% for needs, 30% for wants, and 20% for savings and debt repayment. We'll explore how this guideline can help you find a balance between covering your essentials, enjoying the things that bring you joy, and making steady progress toward your long-term financial goals.

Of course, the 50/30/20 rule is just a starting point. We'll also discuss some common variations on this theme that you can adapt to your own circumstances. For example, if you live in a high cost-of-living area, you might need to adjust your "needs" budget to accommodate pricier housing or transportation costs. Or if you're laser-focused on paying down debt, you might temporarily redirect more of your "wants" money toward your repayment efforts. The key is to find a balance that works for your unique financial situation.

Now, I know what you might be thinking: "This all sounds great, but how do I actually put it into practice?" Don't worry—we've got you covered there, too! In the final section of this chapter, we'll share some handy worksheets and template ideas you can use to bring your budget to life. These tools will help you translate your big-picture goals into a concrete, actionable plan.

Think of these worksheets like a blueprint for your financial dream home. By filling in the details of your income, expenses, and savings targets, you'll gain a clearer picture of where your money is going and where you have room to make adjustments. And just like an architect might use computer-aided design to visualize a building, you can use spreadsheet tools to create a dynamic, interactive budget that you can easily update and adapt over time.

The best part? Creating a budget doesn't have to be a solo endeavor. Just like building a house often involves a team of experts, crafting your financial plan can be a collaborative effort. Whether you're working with a partner, family member, or financial advisor, these worksheets can help facilitate open, honest conversations about your money goals and challenges.

So, are you ready to roll up your sleeves and start designing the budget of your dreams? Great! Let's start by laying the foundation with a clear, customized set of spending categories. Along the way, we'll share plenty of examples, tips, and exercises to help you feel confident and empowered in your budget-building journey.

Remember, your budget is not a restrictive cage but a supportive scaffolding—a structure that helps you build the life you want with intention and purpose. By taking the time to craft a plan that reflects your unique values and goals, you're taking a powerful step toward financial clarity, security, and freedom.

Alright, it's time to grab your metaphorical hard hat and get to work! Let's start by exploring how to set up budget categories that accurately reflect your financial life and priorities.

SETTING UP YOUR CATEGORIES

Creating a budget that truly works for you starts with defining the right spending categories—ones that accurately reflect your unique lifestyle, priorities, and financial goals. By taking the time to customize your budget buckets upfront, you'll be better equipped to track your spending, identify opportunities for savings, and make sure your money is working hard for the things that matter most. Let's walk through the process of setting up your ideal budget categories step by step.

First, start with the big-picture essentials—the spending areas that form the foundation of your financial life. These are the non-negotiable expenses that you need to cover each month to maintain your basic quality of life, such as:

- Housing: This includes your rent or mortgage payment, along with any associated costs like property taxes, insurance, and HOA fees.

- Utilities: Think electricity, gas, water, sewer, and trash services—all the things that keep your home running smoothly.

- Food: This category covers both your grocery bills and any money you spend dining out or ordering in.

- Transportation: If you own a car, this includes your car payment, gas, insurance, and maintenance costs. If you rely on public transit, this category would cover your monthly bus or train pass.

- Healthcare: Don't forget to budget for health insurance premiums, as well as any regular out-of-pocket medical expenses like prescriptions or co-pays.

- Debt payments: If you have any outstanding loans or credit card balances, you'll want to create a dedicated category for those monthly payments to keep you on track.

These essential categories will likely take up a significant portion of your budget, so it's important to be realistic about what you need to allocate to each one to avoid falling behind. A good rule of thumb is to aim for your essentials to take up no more than 50% of your after-tax income, leaving room for savings, discretionary spending, and financial goals.

Next, think about the discretionary spending categories that bring joy and enrichment to your life. These are the "wants" rather than the "needs"—the expenses that you could theoretically live without, but that add value and happiness to your daily experience. Some common examples might include:

- Entertainment: This could include things like movie or concert tickets, streaming service subscriptions, or gaming purchases.

- Hobbies: Whether you love to garden, knit, or collect rare coins, consider creating a category for the supplies and experiences that fuel your passions.

- Travel: If seeing the world is a priority for you, create a dedicated savings bucket for travel expenses like flights, accommodations, and excursions.

- Personal care: Don't forget to budget for the things that help you look and feel your best, like haircuts, spa treatments, or gym memberships.

- Gifts and donations: If generosity is one of your core values, you might set aside a portion of your budget for charitable giving or thoughtful presents for your loved ones.

The key with these discretionary categories is to align your spending with your values and priorities. For example, if you're passionate about health and wellness, you may decide to allocate $150 per month for a gym membership and yoga studio pass, knowing that these are expenses that truly enrich your life. But if you're more of a homebody, that money might be better spent on creating a cozy home theater setup or upgrading your kitchen tools for more cooking adventures.

Once you've identified your core spending categories, consider adding a few forward-looking buckets that align with your longer-term financial goals. For instance, you might create categories like:

- Emergency savings: Aim to gradually build up a safety net of 3-6 months' worth of expenses, so you're prepared for any unexpected disruptions to your income.

- Retirement: Even if it feels far away, now is the time to start socking away money into retirement accounts like a 401(k) or IRA to take advantage of compound interest.

- Big purchases: If you're saving up for a major expense like a down payment on a house or a dream vacation, create a dedicated category to help you track your progress.

- Education: If you're planning to go back to school or invest in professional development courses, factor those tuition and supply costs into your budget.

By treating your financial goals as a key part of your budget (rather than an afterthought), you'll be more likely to make steady progress toward them each month.

As you put your spending categories into action, remember that your budget is meant to be a flexible, evolving tool. Don't be afraid to adjust your allocations as your circumstances and priorities change over time. The goal is to find a balance that allows you to enjoy your life in the present while also making smart choices for your future.

By checking in with your budget regularly and making tweaks as you go, you'll develop a clearer sense of where your money is going and where you might be able to free up extra cash for the things that matter most. Over time, you'll start to see your spending habits as a powerful reflection of your values and goals — a tool for crafting a life that feels authentic and fulfilling to you.

In our next section, we'll explore one popular budgeting framework that can help guide your spending decisions — the 50/30/20 rule. By understanding how to allocate your money across different priority areas, you can create a balanced budget that helps you make the most of every hard-earned dollar.

THE 50/30/20 RULE AND VARIATIONS

When it comes to creating a budget that balances your needs, wants, and long-term financial goals, the 50/30/20 rule is a simple yet powerful framework to keep in mind. Popularized by U.S. Senator Elizabeth Warren in her book "All Your Worth: The Ultimate Lifetime Money Plan," this approach suggests dividing your after-tax income into three main categories: 50% for needs, 30% for wants, and 20% for savings and debt repayment.

Let's break down each of these categories to understand how the 50/30/20 rule works in practice:

- Needs (50%): Half of your budget should go toward covering your essential living expenses—the non-negotiable costs that you must pay each month to maintain a basic standard of living. This includes things like rent or mortgage payments, utilities, groceries, transportation costs, and healthcare premiums. These are the expenses that you can't easily cut back on without making significant lifestyle changes.

- Wants (30%): The next 30% of your budget is allocated for discretionary spending—the things that bring joy and enrichment to your life, but that you could theoretically live without if push came to shove. This includes categories like entertainment, dining out, shopping, hobbies, and travel. While these expenses can certainly add value to your life, they're also the areas where you have the most flexibility to cut back if needed.

- Savings and Debt Repayment (20%): The final 20% of your budget should be dedicated to your financial future—a combination of savings goals (like building an emergency fund or saving for retirement) and paying down existing debt (like credit card balances or student loans). By earmarking a full fifth of your income for these forward-looking categories, you ensure that you're consistently making progress toward your long-term financial health.

To see how the 50/30/20 rule might work in real life, let's consider an example. Imagine you bring home $4,000 per month in after-tax income. Using the 50/30/20 framework, you would aim to allocate your money as follows:

- $2,000 (50% of $4,000) for needs, such as:

- $1,200 for rent

- $300 for groceries

- $150 for utilities

- $200 for car payment and insurance

- $150 for health insurance premiums

- $1,200 (30% of $4,000) for wants, such as:

- $400 for dining out and entertainment

- $200 for shopping and personal care

- $100 for hobbies and recreation

- $500 for travel savings

- $800 (20% of $4,000) for savings and debt, such as:

- $400 for building emergency savings

- $200 for retirement account contributions

- $200 for extra payments toward credit card debt

Of course, these specific dollar amounts and category breakdowns are just an illustration—your actual budget will depend on your unique income, expenses, and financial priorities. The key is to use the 50/30/20 percentages as a guide to make sure you're covering your bases across all three areas.

It's also worth noting that the 50/30/20 rule is just one budgeting approach, and it may not work for everyone. For example, if you live in a high cost-of-living area, you may need to allocate more than 50% of your income to cover basic needs like housing and transportation. Or if you're working to pay off a large amount of debt, you may need to temporarily trim your "wants" budget to free up more cash for debt repayment.

Some variations on the 50/30/20 rule that take these scenarios into account include:

- The 60/20/20 rule: For those with higher essential costs, this approach suggests allocating 60% of your budget to needs, 20% to wants, and 20% to savings and debt.

- The 70/20/10 rule: If you're laser-focused on paying down debt, you might consider putting 70% of your budget toward needs and debt repayment, 20% toward savings, and 10% toward wants.

- The 80/20 rule: If you're working with a very limited income, you may need to focus on covering your needs first and foremost. In this case, you might allocate 80% of your budget to essential costs and 20% to a combination of wants and savings as your budget allows.

Ultimately, the specific percentage breakdown you use is less important than the core principles behind the 50/30/20 rule:

1. Make sure your essential needs are covered first.

2. Align your discretionary spending with the things that bring you the most fulfillment and joy.

3. Always pay yourself first by allocating a meaningful portion of your income to your future goals.

By keeping these guidelines in mind as you build your budget, you can find a balance that works for your unique financial situation and helps you make consistent progress toward the life you want.

Now that we've explored some different budgeting frameworks, let's dive into the hands-on part of the process: creating a customized budget of your very own. In the next section, we'll provide some templates and worksheets you can use to turn your big-picture budget goals into a concrete, actionable plan.

BRING ON THE WORKSHEETS!

Now that you understand the importance of tracking your income and expenses, it's time to put that knowledge into action by creating your very own budget worksheet. Don't worry if you've never done this before—the key is to just dive in and get started, even if it feels a bit daunting at first.

One of the simplest ways to begin is with a fill-in-the-blank template that guides you through the process step by step. This approach takes the guesswork out of budgeting and helps you focus on plugging in the numbers that matter most.

Picture a spreadsheet with pre-labeled rows for different income sources (like your primary job, side hustles, and investments) and expense categories (such as housing, transportation, groceries, and entertainment). Next to each row, there's a blank cell waiting for you to enter the corresponding dollar amount. As you work your way down the sheet, filling in each figure, you'll start to see your financial big picture taking shape right before your eyes.

The beauty of a fill-in-the-blank template is its simplicity and structure. Rather than starting from a blank page and wondering what to include, the worksheet prompts you to consider all the essential elements of your financial life. This helps ensure you don't overlook any key income streams or expense categories that could throw off your budget down the line.

Plus, as you input your numbers and watch the totals calculate automatically, you'll likely experience a growing sense of empowerment and control over your money. There's something deeply satisfying about seeing your financial situation laid out clearly in black and white (or whatever color scheme you choose for your spreadsheet!).

Of course, you don't have to create your budget worksheet entirely from scratch. There are plenty of free, pre-made templates available online from reputable sources like Microsoft Office, Google Sheets, and personal finance websites. These templates often come with helpful built-in formulas and formatting, so all you have to do is plug in your own numbers and let the sheet do the math for you.

Some popular budgeting apps, like Mint and YNAB (You Need A Budget), also offer digital worksheets that sync with your bank accounts and automatically categorize your transactions. This can be a great option if you prefer a more high-tech, automated approach to budgeting. Just be sure to review the categories and make any necessary adjustments to ensure your budget truly reflects your unique financial situation.

Whether you opt for a paper printout or a digital spreadsheet, the key is to choose a format that feels intuitive and easy for you to use. The more comfortable you are with your budgeting tool, the more likely you are to stick with it over time.

As you fill in your worksheet, remember to be as honest and accurate as possible. Resist the temptation to underestimate your expenses or overestimate your income just to make the numbers look better on paper. The goal is to create a realistic, workable budget that you can actually follow in your day-to-day life, not an idealized version that doesn't match your reality.

34

If you get stuck or feel unsure about certain categories, don't hesitate to reach out for guidance. Talk to a trusted friend or family member who has experience with budgeting, or consider scheduling a meeting with a financial advisor or counselor. Sometimes, a fresh set of eyes and an outside perspective can make all the difference in crafting a budget that truly works for you.

Remember, your budget worksheet is a living document that will evolve over time as your financial situation changes. Don't be afraid to make adjustments as needed, whether that means adding new income streams, re-categorizing expenses, or tweaking your savings and debt payoff goals.

The most important thing is to just get started and keep going. By taking that first step and filling in your budget worksheet, you're already well on your way to greater financial awareness and empowerment. In the next chapter, we'll explore how to use your completed worksheet to set achievable, meaningful financial goals for the short and long term. Get ready to turn your numbers into a roadmap toward the future you've always wanted.

YOUR BLUEPRINT FOR FINANCIAL SUCCESS

In the third chapter of our journey, we ventured into the heart of the budgeting process: crafting a spending plan that aligns with your unique goals, values, and lifestyle. We discovered that a well-designed budget is not a restrictive cage, but rather a supportive framework that empowers you to make intentional choices about your money. Let's take a moment to reflect on the key insights and strategies we explored in this pivotal chapter.

One of the foundational lessons was the importance of setting up personalized budget categories. Just like a tailor creates a custom-fitted suit, we learned how to design spending buckets that truly reflect our financial priorities and obligations. By taking the time to thoughtfully allocate our income across essential needs, meaningful wants, and future-focused savings, we lay the groundwork for a budget that is both realistic and fulfilling.

To guide this process, we introduced the 50/30/20 rule—a flexible budgeting framework that suggests dividing your after-tax income into three main categories: 50% for needs, 30% for wants, and 20% for savings and debt repayment. This simple yet powerful tool provides a starting point for balancing your spending and ensuring that your money is working hard for your short-term and long-term goals.

However, we also recognized that the 50/30/20 rule is just a guideline, not a rigid prescription. We explored various adaptations and scenarios that call for adjusting these percentages based on your unique financial situation, such as living in a high cost-of-living area or prioritizing aggressive debt payoff. The key takeaway is that your budget should be a living, breathing document that evolves with your changing circumstances and aspirations.

To help you bring your ideal budget to life, we dove into the power of budgeting worksheets and templates. These handy tools provide a structured, fill-in-the-blank approach to organizing your income, expenses, and savings targets. By using a worksheet as a starting point, you can take the guesswork and overwhelm out of the budgeting process and focus on plugging in the numbers that matter most to you.

But beyond just the practical nuts and bolts, we also emphasized the importance of infusing your budget with a spirit of flexibility, self-compassion, and even fun. Remember, your spending plan is not meant to be a punitive taskmaster, but rather a gentle guide that helps you align your daily choices with your deepest values and dreams. By approaching the process with a mindset of curiosity, experimentation, and growth, you'll be more likely to stick with your budget for the long haul.

As you reflect on these key lessons from Chapter Three, take a moment to celebrate the progress you've made so far. Designing a personalized budget is a significant milestone in your financial journey — one that requires introspection, honesty, and a willingness to get creative. Honor the time and energy you've invested in this process, and trust that it will pay off in greater clarity, confidence, and control over your money.

Looking ahead, the next chapter will challenge you to put your newly minted budget into action by setting clear, achievable financial goals. You'll learn how to translate your big-picture dreams into specific, measurable targets and develop a step-by-step plan for reaching them. With your customized spending plan as a foundation, you'll be well-equipped to start turning your financial aspirations into reality.

So embrace the journey ahead with openness and determination, knowing that each intentional choice you make with your money is a powerful step toward the life you envision. Your dream budget is not a static destination, but a dynamic tool that will grow and evolve with you over time. Trust in the process, stay curious, and keep moving forward—your financial freedom awaits.

CHAPTER FOUR

Setting Goals That Stick, Short-Term and Long-Term

Picture this: It's a year from now, and you're sitting down to review your finances. As you scroll through your bank statements and investment accounts, a huge grin spreads across your face. Staring back at you in black and white are the tangible results of a year's worth of hard work, discipline, and intentional choices. You see a hefty emergency fund that makes you feel safe and secure, a shrinking debt balance that no longer keeps you up at night, and steadily growing retirement accounts that put you right on track for the future of your dreams.

As you reflect on the incredible progress you've made, you can't help but feel a surge of pride, gratitude, and excitement. You think back to a year ago, when your financial goals felt more like distant fantasies than achievable realities. But then you remember the moment when everything changed - the moment you learned to set goals that stick.

In this chapter, we're going to dive into the art and science of effective financial goal-setting. We'll explore how to craft targets that are clear, specific, and deeply meaningful to you - the kind of goals that light a fire in your belly and keep you laser-focused, even when the going gets tough.

First, we'll break down the SMART goal framework and show you how to apply it to your unique financial dreams. SMART stands for Specific, Measurable, Achievable, Relevant, and Time-bound - five key criteria that separate wishy-washy wants from concrete, actionable goals. We'll walk through each of these components and help you turn your big, someday ideas into step-by-step roadmaps for success.

But setting rock-solid goals is just the first piece of the puzzle. To really supercharge your motivation and increase your odds of success, you need to be able to visualize the finish line in vivid detail. That's why we'll also explore some powerful techniques for bringing your financial dreams to life and keeping them at the forefront of your mind. From classic vision boards to high-tech tracking apps, we'll share a smörgåsbord of tools and strategies you can use to stay engaged, inspired, and utterly unstoppable.

Of course, no journey to financial success is complete without a few twists and turns along the way. As you work towards your big, audacious money goals, you'll inevitably face moments when your short-term desires and your long-term vision feel like they're pulling you in opposite directions. That's why we'll also dive into the delicate art of balancing your present wants with your future needs.

We'll explore how to use tools like values-based budgeting and targeted rewards to stay motivated and on track, even when shiny temptations threaten to derail your progress. We'll also share some proven strategies for bouncing back from setbacks and staying the course, no matter what life throws your way.

By the end of this chapter, you'll have a veritable financial goal-setting toolkit at your fingertips - a collection of practical, proven techniques for turning your money dreams into your new reality. You'll know how to set crystal-clear targets that make your heart sing, create vivid mental movies of your success, and navigate the inevitable ups and downs of the journey with grace and resilience.

Best of all, you'll have a newfound sense of clarity, confidence, and control over your financial destiny. No more vague wishes or halfhearted resolutions - just clear, concrete goals and a bullet-proof plan for achieving them, one smart money move at a time.

So grab a notebook, pour yourself a mug of something delicious, and let's dive in! Your future self will thank you for the incredible gift you're about to give them - the gift of goals that stick, no matter what.

CREATING SMART FINANCIAL GOALS

When it comes to setting financial goals, it's not enough to just have a vague idea of what you want to accomplish. To turn your money dreams into reality, you need a clear roadmap to guide your daily choices and keep you motivated for the long haul. That's where the SMART goal-setting framework comes in.

SMART is an acronym that stands for Specific, Measurable, Achievable, Relevant, and Time-bound. Let's break down each of these criteria and explore how they can help you craft financial goals that are both inspiring and attainable.

Specific: A specific goal is one that is clear, focused, and well-defined. Instead of setting a general goal like "save more money," a specific financial goal might be "save $5,000 for a down payment on a car." By getting granular about what exactly you want to achieve, you give yourself a concrete target to work towards and make it easier to track your progress along the way.

Measurable: For a goal to be effective, you need to be able to quantify and track your progress. This means setting benchmarks and milestones that you can use to gauge your success over time. For example, if your goal is to pay off $10,000 in credit card debt, you might break that down into smaller, measurable targets like paying off $800 per month or increasing your monthly payment by $50 each quarter.

Achievable: While it's great to dream big, it's also important to set financial goals that are realistic and attainable given your current resources and circumstances. This doesn't mean you shouldn't challenge yourself, but rather that you should strike a balance between ambition and feasibility. For instance, saving $1 million in a year might not be achievable if you're just starting your career, but saving $5,000 in that same timeframe could be a stretch goal that feels within reach.

Relevant: To stay motivated over the long term, your financial goals need to be aligned with your broader values, priorities, and life vision. In other words, they should be relevant to the big picture of what you want to achieve and experience. For example, if travel is one of your core passions, setting a goal to save $3,000 for a dream vacation might feel more inspiring than a general goal to save $3,000 for a rainy day.

Time-bound: Finally, a SMART financial goal needs to have a clear timeline attached to it. This helps create a sense of urgency and accountability, and gives you a framework for breaking your big goal down into smaller, achievable steps. For example, if you want to save $20,000 for a down payment on a house, you might give yourself a deadline of 3 years to reach that target. From there, you can work backwards to figure out how much you need to save each month or year to stay on track.

Now that we've explored the SMART criteria, let's look at a few examples of how they can be applied to different types of financial goals:

Short-term goal example: "Save $500 for holiday gifts by December 1st."

Notice how this goal is:

- Specific (a defined amount for a specific purpose),

- Measurable ($500 is a clear target),

- Achievable (saving $50-100 per month could make this feasible),

- Relevant (if gift-giving is an important part of your holiday tradition), and

- Time-bound (the December 1st deadline creates a sense of urgency).

Long-term goal example: "Save $1 million for retirement by age 65."

This goal is:

- Specific (a clear amount and purpose),

- Measurable (progress can be tracked over time),

- Achievable (with consistent saving/investing over decades),

- Relevant (financial security is a key part of most people's life vision),

- Time-bound (age 65 provides a defined endpoint)

Of course, with a long-term goal like this, you would also want to break it down into smaller, interim targets along the way. For example, you might set milestone goals like saving your first $100,000 by age 40 or reaching a net worth of $500,000 by age 55.

The beauty of the SMART framework is that it provides a clear, actionable blueprint for setting financial goals that are both meaningful and achievable. By taking the time to think through each of these criteria for your own money aspirations, you can create a personalized roadmap that keeps you anchored, inspired, and consistently moving in the direction of your dreams.

But setting SMART goals is just the first step — to really supercharge your motivation and increase your odds of success, it can be incredibly powerful to visualize what the achievement of your goals will look and feel like. In the next section, we'll explore some creative strategies for bringing your financial goals to life and keeping them front-of-mind as you navigate your day-to-day money choices. Get ready to tap into the power of your imagination and watch your motivation soar!

Visualizing Success

Setting clear, SMART financial goals is a crucial first step in turning your money dreams into reality — but as the old saying goes, "Out of sight, out of mind." To really supercharge your motivation and keep your goals front and center, it can be incredibly powerful to create visual reminders of what you're working towards. By engaging your imagination and tapping into the emotional pull of your aspirations, you can create a tangible roadmap that keeps you inspired and on track, even when the day-to-day grind of budgeting and saving starts to feel like a slog.

One popular tool for goal visualization is the classic vision board. A vision board is simply a collage of images, quotes, and other visual representations of your goals and dreams. The idea is to gather up pictures and words that evoke the feelings and experiences you want to cultivate in your life — whether that's financial security, travel adventures, a dream home, or a sense of abundance and generosity.

To create your own financial vision board, start by setting aside some quiet, reflective time to really dive into the details of your money goals. Ask yourself questions like:

- What does financial success look and feel like to me?

- What experiences do I want my money to enable in the short-term and long-term?

- What kind of lifestyle do I want to create for myself and my loved ones?

- What legacy do I want to leave behind?

As you brainstorm, jot down any images, words, or ideas that come to mind. Maybe financial freedom looks like a serene beach vacation, a passport full of stamps, or the ability to volunteer for causes you care about without worrying about income. Maybe it feels like the security of a fully funded emergency fund, the satisfaction of being debt-free, or the joy of surprising your parents with a special gift or experience.

Once you have a list of ideas, start gathering visuals that represent these goals and feelings. You can flip through magazines, search for images online, or even take your own photos of places, things, or people that inspire you. The key is to choose images that really evoke an emotional response and make your goals feel vivid and real.

Next, arrange your images and words on a poster board, corkboard, or even a dedicated section of your wall. You can add embellishments like stickers, washi tape, or inspiring quotes to make it feel more personal and visually appealing. Then, hang your vision board somewhere where you'll see it often — like your bedroom, office, or even the inside of your closet door.

The beauty of a vision board is that it acts as a constant, tangible reminder of the bigger picture behind your daily financial choices. When you're feeling tempted to splurge on an impulse purchase or skip a savings contribution, you can look at your board and reconnect with the deeper "why" behind your goals. Over time, this visual reinforcement can help reframe your relationship with money from one of scarcity and deprivation to one of abundance, purpose, and joyful anticipation.

Of course, a vision board is just one tool for keeping your financial goals front-of-mind. Another powerful strategy is to use a financial tracker to visualize your progress over time. This could be as simple as a handwritten chart where you color in a box for every $100 you save towards a specific goal, or a more high-tech solution like a budgeting app with built-in goal tracking features.

The key is to choose a tracking method that feels fun, motivating, and visually engaging to you. Some people love the tangible satisfaction of putting pen to paper and watching their progress bar fill up over time. Others prefer the convenience and real-time feedback of a digital tracker. There's no right or wrong approach — the best system is the one you'll actually stick with and enjoy using.

One way to make financial tracking feel more meaningful is to tie it directly to your bigger-picture goals and values. For example, if one of your core aspirations is to be able to give generously to others, you could create a special tracker for your charitable giving goals. Each time you make a donation or volunteer your time, add a sticker, checkmark, or other visual icon to your tracker. Over time, you'll create a powerful visual representation of the impact you're making and the values you're living out through your financial choices.

Another fun way to stay engaged with your financial goals is to use journal prompts for self-reflection and motivation. At the beginning of each month or quarter, take some time to write out your answers to questions like:

- What financial milestones do I want to achieve in the next 30/90 days, and why?

- What did I do well with my money last month/quarter, and what do I want to improve going forward?

- How will achieving my current financial goals help me live out my values and create the life I want?

- What would my future self thank me for doing with my money today?

By regularly checking in with your goals and reflecting on your progress, you can cultivate a sense of clarity, purpose, and momentum that keeps you energized and on track. Plus, when you look back on your journal entries months or years down the line, you'll have a powerful record of how far you've come and the amazing growth you've achieved along the way.

Ultimately, the key to successful financial visualization is to find the tools and techniques that resonate most deeply with you. Whether you're a visual thinker who loves the tactile creativity of a vision board, a data nerd who geeks out over tracking spreadsheets, or a reflective soul who processes best through writing, there's a visualization strategy out there that can help you tap into the emotional power of your goals.

By taking the time to create visual representations of your financial aspirations, you're not just daydreaming about some far-off future — you're actively priming your brain to notice and act on opportunities that align with your vision. You're training yourself to make choices from a place of abundance, purpose, and possibility, rather than scarcity and limitation. Most importantly, you're giving yourself a daily reminder of the incredible life you're building, one small financial choice at a time.

So go ahead — bust out the magazines, markers, and poster board, or fire up that shiny new tracking app on your phone. Give yourself permission to dream big and get creative about what financial success looks like for you. With a clear vision to guide you and a tangible representation of your progress to keep you motivated, there's no limit to what you can achieve with your money.

Now that we've explored the power of visualization, let's dive into the nitty-gritty of turning those big, shiny goals into a practical, actionable plan. In the next section, we'll talk about how to balance your short-term financial milestones with your long-term vision, so you can create a roadmap that keeps you motivated and on track for the long haul.

BALANCING SHORT-TERM WINS AND LONG-TERM VISION

When it comes to managing our money, most of us are juggling a variety of financial priorities at any given time. We might be working towards a big, future-focused goal like saving for a down payment on a house or investing for retirement, while also trying to enjoy life in the present with things like weekends away, dinners out with friends, or the occasional impulse splurge. And of course, we're also trying to keep up with the day-to-day expenses of things like rent, groceries, and utilities. With so many competing demands on our dollars, it's easy to feel like we're constantly playing catch-up or making trade-offs between our present happiness and our future security.

So how can we find a sense of balance and purpose amidst all these swirling financial priorities? How do we stay motivated to chip away at our long-term goals when there are so many shiny temptations vying for our attention (and our wallets) in the here-and-now?

The key is to develop a money management mindset that honors both our current quality of life and our bigger-picture aspirations. Rather than seeing our short-term and long-term goals as an either/or proposition, we can learn to approach them as a both/and — a delicate balancing act that requires intentionality, flexibility, and a hefty dose of self-compassion along the way.

One way to strike this balance is to use the "buckets" approach to budgeting. With this strategy, you divide your money into different categories or "buckets," each with its own specific purpose and timeline. For example, you might have buckets for:

- Essential living expenses (rent, food, transportation, etc.)

- Short-term savings goals (holiday gifts, weekend getaways, etc.)

- Long-term savings goals (down payment fund, retirement investments, etc.)

- Discretionary spending (restaurants, entertainment, shopping, etc.)

- Emergency fund (unexpected expenses, job loss, etc.)

By giving every dollar a job and ensuring that you're allocating some of your income to each of these key areas, you can create a sense of balance and forward momentum in your financial life. You're covering your basic needs, making steady progress on your big goals, and still leaving room for some fun and flexibility along the way.

Of course, this is often easier said than done. In the face of shiny short-term temptations, it can be all too easy to raid our long-term savings buckets or let our discretionary spending spiral out of control. That's why it's so important to get crystal clear on our "why" — the deeper values and motivations driving our financial goals.

Budgeting for Beginners

For example, let's say you're working towards saving $20,000 for a down payment on your first home. When you're in the thick of scrimping and budgeting, it can be tough to stay motivated, especially when your friends are jetting off on Instagram-worthy vacations or splurging on the latest tech gadgets. But if you take the time to really connect with your underlying reasons for wanting to own a home — whether it's the stability of having a place to call your own, the pride of building equity, or the freedom to paint the walls whatever color you darn well please — you'll be far more likely to stay the course when temptation strikes.

One powerful way to keep your "why" front-and-center is to create visual reminders of your long-term goals. This could be as simple as putting a photo of your dream home on your fridge, changing your computer background to an image of the city where you want to retire, or even just jotting down your top financial priorities on a sticky note and posting it above your desk. By surrounding yourself with tangible representations of the life you're working towards, you'll be more likely to pause and reconsider before blowing your budget on an impulse buy.

Another key strategy for balancing short-term and long-term financial priorities is to build in regular rewards along the way. While delayed gratification is an important muscle to flex, it's also crucial to give yourself a pat on the back for the progress you're making, no matter how incremental. This could mean treating yourself to a nice dinner out when you hit a savings milestone, taking a weekend staycation when you pay off a credit card balance, or even just doing a little happy dance every time you resist the siren song of the sale section.

The point is to find small, meaningful ways to celebrate your financial wins, both big and small. This not only helps keep you motivated in the moment, but it also starts to reframe your relationship with money from one of constant struggle and sacrifice to one of joyful progress and possibility.

Of course, there will likely be times when our short-term and long-term goals feel completely at odds with each other — like when we're invited to a destination wedding right as we're trying to max out our retirement contributions for the year. In these moments, it can be helpful to zoom out and take a big-picture view of our financial priorities.

49

Rather than getting bogged down in the minutiae of individual spending decisions, we can ask ourselves questions like:

- What are my non-negotiable financial priorities in this season of life?

- What trade-offs am I willing to make to honor those priorities?

- How can I get creative about satisfying my short-term desires in a way that doesn't derail my long-term progress?

- What would my future self thank me for prioritizing right now?

By taking a values-centered approach to these tough decisions, we can find our way to a middle ground that allows for both present enjoyment and future security. Maybe that means finding a less expensive way to celebrate with the wedding couple, like offering to help with DIY decorations instead of splurging on a pricey hotel room. Or maybe it means saying a gracious "no" to the invitation and resolving to connect with the couple in a more low-key way after the wedding.

Ultimately, learning to balance our short-term and long-term financial goals is a lifelong process of trial and error, adjustment, and growth. It requires us to get radically honest about our values and priorities, to cultivate a spirit of flexibility and creativity in our money choices, and to extend ourselves plenty of grace when we inevitably wobble off course.

The good news is, every small win along the way adds up to massive gains over time. By staying connected to our deeper "why," celebrating our progress, and course-correcting as needed, we can gradually transform our financial lives from a constant tug-of-war to a joyful dance between our present needs and our grandest dreams for the future.

And speaking of those long-term dreams, one of the most powerful tools we have for turning them into reality is a robust savings plan. In the next section, we'll dive into the nuts and bolts of building your financial safety net, with strategies for saving more, stressing less, and sleeping soundly knowing that you're prepared for whatever life throws your way. Get ready to unleash your inner savings superhero!

Dream It, Plan It, Achieve It

In Chapter Four, we embarked on a transformative journey of envisioning, planning, and achieving your short-term and long-term financial aspirations. We discovered that setting clear, compelling goals is the secret sauce that turns your budget from a static spreadsheet into a dynamic roadmap for success. Let's dive into the key insights and strategies that emerged from this illuminating chapter.

First and foremost, we introduced the power of the SMART goal framework — a proven approach to crafting targets that are Specific, Measurable, Achievable, Relevant, and Time-bound. By applying these five criteria to your financial goals, you transform vague wishes into concrete, actionable plans. We explored how to use the SMART framework to set both short-term milestones, like saving for a holiday gift budget, and long-term aspirations, like building a million-dollar retirement nest egg.

But setting compelling goals is just the first piece of the puzzle. To truly supercharge your motivation and increase your likelihood of success, we discovered the importance of visualizing your goals in vivid detail. By creating tangible representations of your financial dreams, like vision boards, progress trackers, or journal prompts, you engage your imagination and emotions in the pursuit of your targets. These powerful visualization techniques help you stay focused, inspired, and connected to your "why" even in the face of challenges or setbacks.

Another key insight from this chapter was the importance of balancing your short-term financial priorities with your long-term vision. We explored strategies for staying motivated and on track when competing desires, like a weekend getaway and a down payment fund, vie for your limited resources. By using tools like values-based budgeting, targeted savings accounts, and regular check-ins, you can ensure that you're making steady progress toward your big-picture goals while still enjoying life's little pleasures along the way.

Throughout this goal-setting journey, we emphasized the importance of maintaining a growth mindset and practicing self-compassion. Setting and pursuing financial goals is not about perfection, but about progress. There will inevitably be setbacks, detours, and moments of frustration along the way. By viewing these challenges as opportunities for learning and recalibration, rather than as failures, you build resilience and adaptability — two essential qualities for long-term financial success.

As you reflect on these key lessons from Chapter Four, take a moment to celebrate the powerful shifts you've made in your relationship with money. By learning to set clear, meaningful goals and stay connected to your financial "why," you've taken a quantum leap toward creating a life of purpose, abundance, and joy. You're no longer just dreaming about your ideal financial future — you're actively designing it, one intentional goal at a time.

Looking ahead, the next chapter will explore the nuts and bolts of building your financial safety net. You'll discover proven strategies for creating an emergency fund, protecting your wealth, and cultivating a sense of financial security that allows you to pursue your goals with confidence and peace of mind. With your SMART goals as your north star, you'll be well-equipped to navigate life's unexpected twists and turns with grace and resilience.

So here's to you, my friend — the architect of your financial destiny. Keep envisioning, keep planning, and keep taking bold, purposeful action toward your dreams. Your future self will thank you for the gifts of clarity, focus, and determination you're cultivating today. Onward and upward!

CHAPTER FIVE

SAVING SECRETS, THE ART OF BUILDING YOUR SAFETY NET

Imagine you're walking a tightrope, high above the ground. Every step is an exhilarating but nerve-wracking experience. Your heart races, your muscles tense, and your focus narrows to the thin wire beneath your feet. Now imagine that same tightrope, but with a safety net stretched out below you. Suddenly, the fear dissipates, replaced by a sense of confidence and freedom. You can enjoy the thrill of the heights, secure in the knowledge that you have a soft place to land if you stumble.

This is the power of an emergency fund - your financial safety net. In a world filled with unexpected twists and turns, having a cushion of savings can transform your relationship with money from one of constant anxiety to one of stability and resilience. With an emergency fund in place, you can navigate life's surprises with grace and flexibility, knowing that you have the resources to catch you if you fall.

In this chapter, we'll explore the art and science of building your emergency fund. We'll start by discussing the essential role this safety net plays in your overall financial health. Just like a well-engineered suspension system smooths out the bumps in the road, your emergency fund absorbs the shocks of unexpected expenses, job losses, or income disruptions. It allows you to stay on track towards your long-term goals, even when life throws you a curveball.

Next, we'll dive into the nuts and bolts of determining your emergency fund target. We'll walk through how to calculate your essential living expenses and translate that into a personalized savings goal. Just like a tailor takes precise measurements to craft a perfectly fitted suit, we'll help you create an emergency fund that is customized to your unique financial situation and risk tolerance.

Of course, knowing your savings target is only half the battle. The real challenge lies in actually building up your emergency fund, especially when you're juggling competing financial priorities. That's why we'll spend a significant portion of this chapter exploring proven strategies for making saving money an automatic, painless part of your routine.

We'll discuss how to set up automated transfers that quietly siphon a portion of your income into your savings account, like a hidden pipeline steadily filling a reservoir. We'll explore the power of payroll deductions and roundup apps that make saving as effortless as breathing. By the end of this section, you'll have a toolbox full of techniques for putting your savings on autopilot.

But building your emergency fund is not just about mechanics - it's also a matter of mindset. Throughout this chapter, we'll discuss the importance of cultivating a savings mentality. We'll explore how small changes in your daily habits, like bringing your lunch to work or cancelling unused subscriptions, can add up to big wins for your emergency fund over time. We'll also tackle the emotional side of saving, offering strategies for staying motivated and celebrating your progress along the way.

Our ultimate goal is to help you develop a savings muscle that grows stronger with each repetition. Just like an athlete trains consistently to build endurance and power, we'll show you how to flex your savings skills on a regular basis, gradually increasing your capacity to save over time. With practice and persistence, building your emergency fund will shift from a daunting chore to an empowering ritual - one that affirms your commitment to your financial well-being with every automated transfer.

By the end of this chapter, you'll have a clear roadmap for constructing your financial safety net, one paycheck at a time. You'll understand the why, the what, and the how of emergency fund saving. But more importantly, you'll have the confidence and motivation to put these strategies into action in your own life.

Remember, building an emergency fund is not an overnight journey - it's a gradual, steady climb towards financial resilience. There will be setbacks and plateaus along the way, but with the right tools and mindset, you have the power to create a savings cushion that can weather any storm. So take a deep breath, trust in the process, and get ready to discover the life-changing magic of a well-stocked emergency fund. Your future self will thank you.

Emergency Fund Essentials

An emergency fund is your financial safety net, a critical tool in your budgeting arsenal that can protect you from life's unexpected curveballs. Think of it as a shock absorber for your finances—when an unforeseen expense or income disruption hits, your emergency fund softens the blow, allowing you to navigate the challenge without derailing your long-term financial goals.

So, why is an emergency fund so vital? Let's break it down. Imagine your car suddenly needs a costly repair, your roof springs a leak, or you face a medical emergency. Without an emergency fund to fall back on, you might be forced to rely on high-interest credit cards, dip into your long-term savings, or even borrow money from friends or family. These stop-gap measures can lead to a cycle of debt, erode your hard-earned savings, and strain your relationships.

In contrast, having a well-stocked emergency fund empowers you to handle these surprises with confidence and stability. Instead of scrambling for funds or compromising your future, you can tap into your emergency reserves, cover the expense, and move forward without missing a beat.

Now, you might be wondering, "How much should I save in my emergency fund?" While the exact amount varies based on your unique circumstances, a good rule of thumb is to set aside enough to cover three to six months' worth of essential living expenses. This includes costs like housing, food, utilities, transportation, and insurance—the bare necessities to keep your life running smoothly.

To determine your personalized emergency fund target, start by adding up your essential monthly expenses. Then, multiply that figure by the number of months you want to cover (aim for at least three, but six is even better). The result is your emergency fund goal.

For example, let's say your essential monthly expenses total $2,000. To build a three-month emergency fund, you'd need to save $6,000 ($2,000 x 3). For a six-month fund, your target would be $12,000 ($2,000 x 6).

Looking at those numbers, you might feel overwhelmed, especially if you're starting from scratch. But here's the good news: you don't have to build your emergency fund overnight. The key is to start small and be consistent.

Begin by setting aside a portion of your income each month, no matter how modest. Even $50 or $100 per month can add up over time. As you get more comfortable with budgeting and find ways to trim expenses or boost your income, you can gradually increase your contributions.

Another strategy is to automate your savings. Set up a separate savings account for your emergency fund and arrange for a fixed amount to be transferred from your checking account each payday. By making your contributions automatic, you'll build your fund steadily without having to remember or be tempted to skip a month.

As you watch your emergency fund grow, resist the urge to tap into it for non-emergencies. Remember, this money is a safeguard, not a piggy bank for impulse purchases. By preserving your emergency fund for true crises, you'll maintain a strong financial foundation that can weather any storm.

Building an emergency fund is a crucial step in your budgeting journey, one that offers peace of mind and financial resilience. By understanding its importance, setting a personalized savings target, and contributing consistently, you'll create a robust safety net that protects you through life's ups and downs. In the next section, we'll explore how automating your savings can supercharge your emergency fund growth, making the process even more effortless and effective.

AUTOMATING YOUR SAVINGS

Automating your savings is a game-changer when it comes to building your emergency fund and reaching your financial goals. By setting up automatic transfers, enrolling in payroll deductions, or using round-up apps, you can make saving money an effortless part of your routine, almost like putting your savings on autopilot.

Let's dive into the benefits of automating your savings. First and foremost, it takes the guesswork and temptation out of the equation. When you automate your savings, you're ensuring that a portion of your income is consistently directed towards your emergency fund or other savings goals, without you having to remember or make the decision each month. This way, your savings grow steadily in the background, even if you're busy with life's other demands.

Automatic transfers are a simple yet powerful tool. You can set up a recurring transfer from your checking account to your savings account, timed to coincide with your payday or any other regular interval. By moving money to your savings before you have a chance to spend it, you're prioritizing your financial future and reducing the risk of overspending or neglecting your savings.

Payroll deductions are another convenient option, especially if your employer offers this service. With payroll deductions, a fixed amount or percentage of your paycheck is automatically deposited into your designated savings account before the money even reaches your checking account. This "set it and forget it" approach ensures that your savings grow with each paycheck, without any extra effort on your part.

Round-up apps are a newcomer to the automated savings scene, but they ve quickly gained popularity for their innovative approach. These apps, such as Acorns or Chime, link to your debit or credit card and round up each transaction to the nearest dollar, transferring the spare change to your savings account. For example, if you buy a coffee for $3.50, the app would round the purchase up to $4.00 and move the extra $0.50 into your savings. While these small amounts might seem insignificant, they can add up quickly over time, especially if you make numerous transactions throughout the month.

The beauty of automated savings lies in its simplicity and consistency. By making saving a regular, automated habit, you're more likely to stick with it and see your emergency fund and other savings grow over time. Plus, by removing the manual effort and decision-making, you'll be less tempted to skip a contribution or divert the money elsewhere.

If you're new to automating your savings, start small and gradually increase your contributions as you adjust to the new flow of your finances. Even a small amount, like $20 or $50 per paycheck, can make a big difference over the long run. As you get more comfortable with the process and start seeing your savings balance grow, you can challenge yourself to increase your automated contributions, accelerating your progress towards your emergency fund target and other financial milestones.

Remember, automating your savings is not about depriving yourself or sacrificing your current lifestyle. Instead, it's about making a simple shift in how you manage your money, ensuring that your future financial security is always a priority. By embracing the power of automation, you're taking a proactive step towards building a solid financial foundation, one that can support you through life's unexpected challenges and help you achieve your long-term goals.

As you set up your automated savings plan, be sure to choose a savings account with a competitive interest rate, so your money can grow even faster. And don't forget to celebrate your progress along the way—each automated transfer or payroll deduction is a small victory, bringing you one step closer to financial peace of mind.

In the next section, we'll explore some best practices for maintaining a consistent savings habit and optimizing your emergency fund growth over time. With the power of automation on your side, you'll be well on your way to building a robust financial safety net that can weather any storm.

BEST PRACTICES FOR CONSISTENT GROWTH

Now that you've set up your automated savings plan and are watching your emergency fund grow, let's explore some best practices for maintaining your momentum and optimizing your savings growth over time. By making small, strategic changes to your savings habits, you can accelerate your progress and reach your financial goals even faster.

One of the most effective ways to boost your savings is to gradually increase your automated contributions. As you become more comfortable with your budgeting process and start seeing the benefits of your growing emergency fund, consider challenging yourself to save a little more each month.

For example, let's say you started by automatically transferring $50 from your checking account to your savings account each payday. After a few months, you might find that you've adjusted to this new cash flow and have a bit more wiggle room in your budget. At this point, consider increasing your automated transfer to $60 or $75 per payday. While the increase might seem small, it can add up significantly over time.

To illustrate, imagine you're paid bi-weekly and initially save $50 per paycheck, which equates to $1,300 saved annually ($50 x 26 paychecks). If you increase your contribution to $75 per paycheck, your annual savings would jump to $1,950 ($75 x 26 paychecks) — an extra $650 saved each year. Over five years, that small $25 increase per paycheck would result in an additional $3,250 in your emergency fund, not including any interest earned.

Another strategy to grow your savings is to allocate a portion of any windfalls or extra income to your emergency fund. This could include tax refunds, bonuses, overtime pay, or even money saved by reducing expenses like canceling an unused subscription or negotiating a better rate on your phone bill. By directing these extra funds to your savings, you can give your emergency fund a boost without putting additional strain on your regular budget.

Consistency is key when it comes to building your savings. Try to avoid the temptation to skip or reduce your automated contributions, even if you have a month with unexpected expenses or reduced income. By maintaining your savings habit through both good times and challenging ones, you'll develop the discipline and resilience needed to reach your long-term financial goals.

It's also important to regularly review and adjust your savings plan as your financial situation evolves. As you get raises, change jobs, or pay off debts, consider increasing your automated savings contributions to reflect your new circumstances. By continuously updating your savings strategy, you'll ensure that you're always making progress towards your emergency fund target and other financial milestones.

Finally, don't forget to celebrate your progress along the way. Building a robust emergency fund takes time and dedication, and each milestone you reach deserves recognition. Whether you've saved your first $500, reached the halfway point to your goal, or finally achieved your three-to-six-month emergency fund target, take a moment to appreciate how far you've come and the financial security you've created for yourself.

Remember, building your emergency fund is not a race, but a journey. By consistently applying these best practices and maintaining a patient, disciplined approach, you'll develop strong savings habits that will serve you well throughout your financial life. As you watch your emergency fund grow, you'll gain the peace of mind that comes with knowing you're prepared for whatever challenges life may bring.

In the next chapter, we'll dive into the world of debt—understanding the different types, developing strategies to reduce and eliminate it, and exploring how managing debt effectively can accelerate your progress towards financial freedom.

YOUR SAVINGS SUPERPOWER

In the preceding sections of this chapter, we've explored the essential components of building a robust financial safety net. We started by discussing the crucial role an emergency fund plays in protecting you from life's unexpected challenges, like job loss, medical emergencies, or major home repairs. Just as a well-engineered suspension system allows a car to handle bumps and potholes smoothly, your emergency fund acts as a shock absorber for your finances, helping you navigate difficult times without derailing your long-term goals.

Next, we delved into strategies for making the savings process as effortless and painless as possible. By setting up automatic transfers from your checking account to a dedicated emergency fund savings account, you can steadily grow your financial cushion without having to think about it on a day-to-day basis. We also discussed how payroll deductions and round-up apps can make saving feel almost invisible, quietly siphoning small amounts into your safety net while you focus on other aspects of your financial life.

Finally, we explored best practices for optimizing your emergency fund growth over time. This includes gradually increasing your automated savings contributions, allocating windfalls or extra income to your fund, and regularly reviewing your plan to ensure it aligns with your evolving needs and circumstances. By approaching your emergency fund with consistency, patience, and a commitment to incremental progress, you can build a savings cushion that provides both financial stability and peace of mind.

As we've seen throughout this chapter, developing a robust emergency fund is a transformative habit that can reshape your relationship with money. When you know you have a financial safety net to catch you during tough times, you can approach your day-to-day money management with a greater sense of confidence, clarity, and purpose. Instead of operating from a place of scarcity and fear, you can make financial decisions that align with your values and long-term goals.

But the benefits of a healthy savings habit extend far beyond just your emergency fund. By flexing your savings muscles on a regular basis, you're developing a powerful skill set that can serve you in countless areas of your financial life. Whether you're saving for a down payment on a house, building a vacation fund, or investing for retirement, the same principles of consistency, automation, and incremental progress will be your allies on the journey.

In essence, your ability to save is like a financial superpower—a force that allows you to shape your monetary destiny and create the life you desire. Just as a superhero's abilities grow stronger with training and practice, your savings skills will become more robust and automatic over time. And as you watch your emergency fund and other savings grow, you'll likely find yourself feeling more empowered, resilient, and in control of your financial narrative.

Of course, saving is just one piece of the larger financial puzzle. To truly harness your money superpowers, it's also crucial to develop smart strategies for managing debt. In the next chapter, we'll dive into the world of debt repayment, exploring how to distinguish between "good" and "bad" debt, accelerate your debt elimination using methods like the debt snowball and debt avalanche, and cultivate the motivation and resilience to stay the course on your debt-free journey. By combining a robust savings habit with a proactive approach to debt management, you'll be well on your way to becoming the hero of your own financial story.

CHAPTER SIX

TAMING THE DEBT BEAST, STRATEGIES TO REDUCE AND ELIMINATE

Picture this: you're standing face to face with a towering, snarling beast. Its eyes glow with an eerie, menacing light, and its gaping jaws drip with the remnants of your hard-earned cash. This is no ordinary monster - it's the Debt Beast, and it's been feeding on your financial dreams for far too long.

If this imagery resonates with you, you're not alone. For many people, debt can feel like an overwhelming, insurmountable adversary - a relentless force that devours their income, haunts their dreams, and keeps them trapped in a cycle of financial stress and struggle. But here's the good news: with the right strategies, tools, and mindset, you can tame this beast and reclaim control of your financial life.

In this chapter, we'll arm you with the knowledge and skills you need to conquer your debt, once and for all. We'll start by shining a light on the different types of debt and how to distinguish between "good debt" and "bad debt." Just like a skilled monster hunter studies their prey, understanding the nature of your debt is the first step in devising an effective plan to defeat it.

Next, we'll introduce you to two powerful debt-slaying weapons: the Debt Snowball and Debt Avalanche methods. These strategies are like silver bullets in your financial arsenal, helping you target your debts with laser-like precision and efficiency. We'll walk you through each approach step by step, so you can choose the one that best fits your unique debt-slaying style.

But vanquishing the Debt Beast isn't just about tactics and numbers - it's also a mental and emotional game. That's why we'll also focus on strategies for staying motivated and energized throughout your debt payoff journey. We'll explore how to celebrate your victories, learn from your setbacks, and keep your eyes on the prize, even when the road ahead feels long and winding.

Imagine this: with each debt you slay, you'll feel a surge of pride and empowerment, like a valiant knight standing tall over a vanquished foe. As your debt balances dwindle and your financial confidence grows, you'll start to see a new horizon emerging - one where you're free to chase your dreams, build your wealth, and live life on your own terms.

By the end of this chapter, you'll have a full arsenal of weapons and strategies to help you tame your Debt Beast and emerge victorious. You'll know how to distinguish between different types of debt, choose a repayment approach that works for you, and stay motivated and inspired along the way.

But more than that, you'll have a newfound sense of hope and determination. You'll know that no matter how fierce your Debt Beast may seem, you have the power within you to conquer it, one dollar at a time. With each payment made and each balance eliminated, you'll be proving to yourself that you're stronger than your debt - that you're the hero of your own financial story.

So sharpen your pencil, summon your courage, and let's dive in. Your debt-free future awaits, and it all starts with understanding the battlefield. In the next section, we'll explore the difference between "good debt" and "bad debt," and how to prioritize your debt-slaying efforts for maximum impact. Get ready to take back your financial kingdom, one vanquished debt at a time.

UNDERSTANDING 'GOOD DEBT' VS. 'BAD DEBT'

When it comes to managing your finances and working towards your goals, not all debt is created equal. Some forms of debt, like mortgages or student loans, can be considered "good debt"—strategic investments in your future that have the potential to generate long-term value. On the other hand, high-interest consumer debt, such as credit card balances or payday loans, is often labeled "bad debt," as it can quickly spiral out of control and derail your financial progress.

Let's dive deeper into the concept of "good debt" and explore why certain types of loans can be viewed as investments. When you take out a mortgage to purchase a home, you're not just buying a place to live—you're also investing in an asset that has the potential to appreciate in value over time. As you pay down your mortgage, you're building equity in your home, which can be a powerful tool for building long-term wealth.

To illustrate this point, let's consider an example. Imagine you purchase a home for $200,000 with a 30-year fixed-rate mortgage at 3.5% interest. Each month, a portion of your mortgage payment goes towards paying down your loan principal, increasing your home equity. Over time, as you continue to make payments and your home value appreciates, your net worth grows. In this sense, your mortgage is a form of forced savings, helping you build wealth through homeownership.

Similarly, educational loans, such as student loans or vocational training loans, can be viewed as investments in your human capital. By financing your education, you're gaining knowledge, skills, and qualifications that can increase your earning potential and open up new career opportunities. While student loans do come with the burden of debt, the long-term financial benefits of a higher education often outweigh the costs.

For example, let's say you take out $50,000 in student loans to earn a bachelor's degree in a high-demand field like computer science or engineering. Upon graduation, you land a job with a starting salary of $75,000 per year. Even with your student loan payments, your increased earning power can help you achieve a higher standard of living and reach your financial goals more quickly than if you hadn't invested in your education.

Now, let's shift gears and examine the other side of the coin: "bad debt." High-interest consumer debt, such as credit card balances, personal loans, or payday loans, is often considered "bad debt" because it can quickly accumulate and become a major financial burden.

Unlike mortgages or student loans, which are typically used to finance appreciating assets or investments in your future, consumer debt is often used to purchase depreciating assets or cover short-term expenses. For example, if you use a credit card to buy a new TV or finance a vacation, you're not only paying for the cost of the item or experience but also the high interest charges that come with carrying a balance.

To put this into perspective, let's say you have a credit card with a $5,000 balance and an annual interest rate of 18%. If you only make the minimum payment each month (typically around 2% of the balance), it would take you over 30 years to pay off the debt, and you'd end up paying over $7,000 in interest charges alone. In this scenario, the high-interest debt is not only costing you money but also preventing you from using those funds to save, invest, or work towards your other financial goals.

So, how can you tackle "bad debt" aggressively? The key is to prioritize paying off your high-interest debts as quickly as possible. One effective strategy is the debt avalanche method, where you focus on paying off your debts in order of interest rate, starting with the highest-interest debt first. By attacking your most expensive debts first, you can minimize the amount of interest you pay over time and accelerate your progress towards becoming debt-free.

Another approach is the debt snowball method, where you focus on paying off your debts in order of balance size, starting with the smallest debt first. While this strategy may not be as mathematically optimal as the debt avalanche method, it can provide a powerful psychological boost by helping you achieve quick wins and build momentum as you work towards tackling your larger debts.

Regardless of which strategy you choose, the key is to make debt repayment a priority in your budget. Look for ways to cut expenses, increase your income, or both, so you can allocate more money towards your debt repayment efforts. As you make progress and see your balances shrink, you'll gain confidence and motivation to keep pushing forward.

In summary, understanding the difference between "good debt" and "bad debt" is crucial for making informed financial decisions. While mortgages and educational loans can be viewed as strategic investments in your future, high-interest consumer debt should be tackled aggressively to minimize its impact on your financial well-being. By prioritizing debt repayment and making smart choices about when and how to use debt, you can take control of your finances and pave the way for a brighter financial future.

In the next section, we'll take a closer look at two popular debt repayment strategies—the debt snowball and debt avalanche methods—and explore how you can use them to accelerate your journey towards becoming debt-free.

Snowball vs. Avalanche Methods

When it comes to tackling debt, two popular repayment strategies have emerged as go-to methods for many people: the debt snowball and the debt avalanche. Both approaches can be effective in helping you become debt-free, but they prioritize different aspects of the debt repayment process. Let's dive into each method, explore their pros and cons, and walk through a simple example to illustrate how they work in practice.

First, let's take a closer look at the debt snowball method. With this approach, you focus on paying off your debts in order of balance size, starting with the smallest debt first. Here's how it works:

1. Make a list of all your debts, excluding your mortgage, and order them from smallest balance to largest.

2. Continue making the minimum payments on all your debts except the smallest one.

3. Allocate as much extra money as possible towards paying off the smallest debt until it's fully paid off.

4. Once the smallest debt is eliminated, take the amount you were paying towards that debt and apply it to the next smallest balance, in addition to its minimum payment.

5. Repeat this process, "snowballing" your payments as you eliminate each debt, until you're completely debt-free.

The primary advantage of the debt snowball method is the psychological boost it provides. By prioritizing your smallest debts first, you can achieve quick wins and build momentum as you see debts disappear from your list. This sense of progress can be highly motivating, keeping you engaged and committed to the repayment process.

However, the debt snowball method has one main drawback: it doesn't take interest rates into account. By focusing solely on balance size, you may end up paying more in interest over time compared to other repayment strategies.

Now, let's explore the debt avalanche method. With this approach, you prioritize paying off your debts in order of interest rate, starting with the highest-interest debt first. Here's how it works:

1. Make a list of all your debts, excluding your mortgage, and order them from highest interest rate to lowest.

2. Continue making the minimum payments on all your debts except the one with the highest interest rate.

3. Allocate as much extra money as possible towards paying off the debt with the highest interest rate until it's fully paid off.

4. Once the highest-interest debt is eliminated, take the amount you were paying towards that debt and apply it to the debt with the next highest interest rate, in addition to its minimum payment.

5. Repeat this process, "avalanching" your payments as you eliminate each debt, until you're completely debt-free.

The main advantage of the debt avalanche method is its mathematical efficiency. By targeting your most expensive debts first, you can minimize the amount of interest you pay over time, potentially saving you money in the long run.

However, the debt avalanche method may require more patience and discipline than the debt snowball approach. Because your highest-interest debts may also have larger balances, it can take longer to see progress and achieve those initial quick wins that the debt snowball method provides.

To illustrate these concepts, let's walk through a simple example. Imagine you have the following debts:

- Credit Card A: $5,000 balance, 18% interest rate

- Credit Card B: $2,000 balance, 15% interest rate

- Personal Loan: $8,000 balance, 10% interest rate

Using the debt snowball method, you would focus on paying off Credit Card B first, as it has the smallest balance. Once that's paid off, you'd move on to Credit Card A, and finally, the Personal Loan.

Using the debt avalanche method, you would start by focusing on Credit Card A, as it has the highest interest rate. Once that's paid off, you'd move on to Credit Card B, and lastly, the Personal Loan.

Both methods can be effective, and the best approach for you will depend on your unique financial situation and personal preferences. Some people find the psychological benefits of the debt snowball method more compelling, while others prefer the mathematical advantage of the debt avalanche approach.

Ultimately, the key is to choose a method that resonates with you and stick with it. Consistency and dedication are essential, regardless of which repayment strategy you choose. As you make progress and see your debts disappear, you'll gain confidence and motivation to keep pushing forward until you reach your goal of becoming debt-free.

Remember, too, that these methods aren't mutually exclusive. You can start with the debt snowball method to build momentum and achieve some quick wins, then transition to the debt avalanche approach to optimize your repayment process and save on interest over the long haul.

As you work towards eliminating your debt, don't forget to celebrate your progress along the way. Each debt you pay off is a significant milestone and a testament to your hard work and dedication. Keeping a positive outlook and maintaining motivation throughout the process will be key to your success.

In the next section, we'll explore some strategies for staying motivated and on track as you work towards becoming debt-free, even when faced with setbacks or challenges.

STAYING MOTIVATED THROUGH THE PAYOFF JOURNEY

Staying motivated throughout your debt repayment journey is just as important as choosing the right strategy. Paying off debt can be a long and sometimes difficult process, but by celebrating your progress, tracking your milestones, and keeping your end goal in sight, you can maintain the momentum and enthusiasm needed to see it through to the end.

One powerful way to stay motivated is to set clear, achievable milestones along your debt repayment path. These milestones can be based on total debt reduction, like celebrating each $1,000 or $5,000 paid off, or they can be tied to specific debts, like throwing a small celebration each time you eliminate a credit card balance or loan. By breaking your larger goal into smaller, more manageable steps, you can experience a sense of progress and achievement throughout the process, rather than waiting until the very end to celebrate.

Tracking your progress visually can also be a great motivator. Consider creating a debt repayment tracker, either on paper or using a spreadsheet or app, where you can record your starting balances, payments made, and remaining debts. As you update your tracker each month, you'll be able to see your debts steadily decreasing, providing a tangible reminder of your hard work and dedication. You might even create a visual representation of your progress, like a debt thermometer or a pie chart that you color in as you pay off each portion of your debt.

Another way to stay motivated is to reward yourself for reaching significant milestones. These rewards don't have to be expensive or extravagant – the key is to choose something that feels meaningful and celebratory to you. For example, after paying off your first credit card, you might treat yourself to a nice dinner out or a small splurge that you've been eyeing. As you reach larger milestones, like paying off half your total debt or eliminating your highest-interest balance, consider planning a weekend getaway or a special outing with loved ones. By incorporating positive reinforcement into your debt repayment journey, you'll associate progress with feelings of accomplishment and enjoyment, fueling your motivation to keep going.

It can also be incredibly motivating to connect with others who are on similar debt repayment journeys. Seek out online forums, social media groups, or even in-person meetups where you can share your experiences, challenges, and triumphs with others who understand what you're going through. Seeing others succeed in paying off their debts can provide inspiration and encouragement, reminding you that your goals are achievable with persistence and dedication.

Sometimes, the most powerful motivation comes from envisioning the life you'll have once you're debt-free. Take some time to think about the positive changes you'll experience when you're no longer burdened by debt. Will you be able to save more for retirement, travel more often, or start that business you've been dreaming of? Will you experience less stress and anxiety, knowing that you're in control of your finances? Hold onto these visions and use them as a source of inspiration when the debt repayment process feels challenging.

Finally, remember that setbacks and obstacles are a normal part of any journey, including debt repayment. If you encounter unexpected expenses, reduced income, or simply a month where you can't make as much progress as you'd hoped, don't be discouraged. These challenges are temporary, and by staying committed to your goal and adjusting your plan as needed, you can overcome them and continue moving forward.

To illustrate the positive impact of becoming debt-free, let's look at a couple of short success stories:

Sarah, a recent college graduate, found herself with $25,000 in credit card debt and student loans. By creating a budget, cutting expenses, and using the debt snowball method, she was able to pay off all her debt in just three years. Today, Sarah is able to save more than 20% of her income each month, and she's planning a trip to Europe to celebrate her newfound financial freedom.

Mark and Lisa, a married couple in their 40s, had accumulated over $50,000 in credit card debt and car loans. By working together, taking on side hustles, and using the debt avalanche method, they were able to eliminate their debt in five years. Now, they're able to focus on saving for their children's college educations and their own retirement, with the peace of mind that comes from being debt-free.

These stories demonstrate that becoming debt-free is not only possible but also incredibly rewarding. By staying motivated, celebrating your progress, and keeping your end goal in sight, you can achieve the same kind of success and financial freedom in your own life.

Remember, your debt repayment journey is unique to you, and progress is progress, no matter how small it may seem. Every dollar you pay towards your debts is a step in the right direction, bringing you closer to the life you want to live. By staying committed, focusing on your milestones, and celebrating your victories along the way, you'll find the motivation and determination needed to see your debt repayment journey through to its successful conclusion.

In the next chapter, we'll shift gears and explore the world of frugal living – learning how to cut expenses, live within your means, and accelerate your debt repayment and savings goals without feeling deprived or overwhelmed.

DEBT-FREE AND THRIVING

In our journey through the landscape of personal finance, we've explored many crucial aspects of budgeting, saving, and intentional living. We've seen how developing a healthy savings habit can provide a sturdy financial safety net, empowering us to weather life's unexpected storms with greater resilience. We've also discovered the transformative power of frugality—how aligning our spending with our deepest values can enrich our lives in ways that go beyond mere monetary gain.

But there's another essential piece of the financial wellness puzzle that we have yet to address head-on: the challenge of managing and eliminating debt. For many people, debt can feel like a hulking, inescapable presence, casting a shadow over their financial lives. Whether it's credit card balances, student loans, or medical bills, the burden of debt can create a sense of overwhelm and hopelessness, making it difficult to envision a path to lasting financial freedom.

However, as we've learned throughout this chapter, debt doesn't have to be a life sentence. With the right strategies, mindset, and support, anyone can develop the skills and resilience to overcome even the most daunting financial obstacles. The journey to debt freedom is not always easy, but it is undeniably worthwhile—not just for the tangible rewards of financial stability, but for the profound sense of empowerment and self-mastery that comes from taking control of your money story.

One of the key insights we've gleaned is the importance of distinguishing between "good" debt and "bad" debt. Not all borrowing is created equal, and understanding the difference can help us make more strategic, purposeful decisions about when and how to use debt in our financial lives.

"Good" debt, such as mortgages or student loans, is often used to finance appreciating assets or investments in our future earning potential. While these obligations still require careful management, they can be valuable tools for building long-term wealth and security when used wisely.

In contrast, "bad" debt, like high-interest credit card balances or payday loans, typically stems from consumption spending that doesn't generate lasting value. This type of debt can quickly spiral out of control, eroding our financial health and hindering our ability to save and invest for the future.

By learning to recognize these distinctions and prioritize the strategic use of debt, we can start to break free from the cycle of endless payments and mounting interest charges. This might involve tactics like consolidating high-interest balances, negotiating with creditors for better terms, or simply committing to paying more than the minimum each month.

Another powerful strategy we've explored is the use of targeted debt repayment methods, such as the debt snowball and debt avalanche. These approaches provide a clear, actionable plan for tackling debt systematically, harnessing the power of small wins and building momentum over time.

The debt snowball method, for example, involves paying off debts from smallest to largest balance, regardless of interest rates. This can be a highly motivating approach, as the quick victories of eliminating smaller debts can provide a sense of progress and encouragement to keep going.

The debt avalanche, on the other hand, prioritizes paying off debts with the highest interest rates first. While this method may take longer to yield noticeable results, it can be more efficient in the long run, as it minimizes the total interest paid over the course of the debt repayment journey.

Whichever method resonates most, the key is to commit to a plan and stay consistent. As we've seen from countless real-life success stories, the path to debt freedom is paved with small, deliberate choices made day after day. It's about finding ways to trim expenses, boost income, and redirect those extra resources towards our debt repayment goals.

But perhaps the most profound lesson we've learned is that the journey to debt freedom is as much an emotional and psychological process as it is a financial one. It's about cultivating a mindset of abundance, gratitude, and self-compassion, even in the face of setbacks and challenges. It's about rewriting our internal narratives around money, letting go of shame and self-judgment, and embracing a vision of a brighter financial future.

By surrounding ourselves with supportive communities, celebrating our progress, and staying focused on our deepest values and aspirations, we can find the strength and resilience to keep moving forward, one payment at a time. Gradually, as we watch our balances dwindle and our financial confidence grow, we'll start to see a new horizon emerging — one where debt is no longer a limitation, but a launching pad for a life of greater freedom, purpose, and joy.

As we continue on this transformative journey, we'll next explore how the principles of intentional living and conscious spending can further enhance our financial wellbeing. In the coming chapter, we'll discuss strategies for aligning our daily money choices with our deepest values, finding contentment in simplicity, and crafting a life that is truly rich in every sense of the word. By combining the skills of debt elimination with a mindful approach to money management, we'll be well-equipped to not just survive, but thrive, on the path to lasting financial freedom.

CHAPTER SEVEN

LIVING FRUGALLY WITHOUT FEELING DEPRIVED

Embarking on a frugal lifestyle can feel daunting at first, especially if you're accustomed to a certain level of spending. You might worry that cutting back on expenses means giving up the things you enjoy, leading to a life of constant sacrifice and deprivation. However, the reality is quite the opposite.

Embracing frugality is not about depriving yourself of joy and comfort, but rather about making intentional choices that align with your values and long-term goals. It's about recognizing that true fulfillment comes not from material possessions or fleeting indulgences, but from living a life of purpose, connection, and financial security.

In this chapter, we'll explore practical strategies for living frugally without feeling like you're missing out. We'll start with simple, actionable "frugal hacks" that you can implement today to start saving money and reducing waste. From savvy shopping tips to creative ways to enjoy free entertainment, these small changes can add up to significant savings over time.

Next, we'll dive into the world of meal planning and lifestyle tweaks. Food is often one of the biggest expenses in any household budget, but it's also an area where small changes can make a big impact. By learning how to plan your meals, shop strategically, and make the most of your ingredients, you can eat well on a budget without sacrificing taste or nutrition. We'll also explore other lifestyle changes, like embracing DIY projects and finding free or low-cost alternatives to expensive hobbies and activities.

Finally, we'll delve into the power of mindset shifts for sustainable saving. Frugal living is not just about changing your external behaviors, but also about transforming your internal relationship with money and consumption. By reframing the idea of "sacrifice" as an investment in your future, cultivating gratitude for what you already have, and finding fulfillment in experiences rather than things, you can develop a more positive, abundant mindset that supports your frugal lifestyle long-term.

Throughout this chapter, we'll emphasize that frugal living is not about deprivation, but about empowerment. By taking control of your spending, prioritizing what matters most to you, and finding creative ways to stretch your resources, you'll not only save money, but also cultivate a deeper sense of contentment, resilience, and freedom in your life.

So whether you're just starting your frugal journey or looking for new ways to deepen your commitment to sustainable living, this chapter will provide you with the tools, insights, and inspiration you need to thrive on less. Let's dive in and discover the joy and abundance that awaits you on the other side of frugality.

In the first section, we'll explore some simple, practical "frugal hacks" that you can start implementing today to kickstart your savings and reduce waste in your daily life.

FRUGAL HACKS YOU CAN START TODAY

Living frugally doesn't have to mean depriving yourself or constantly feeling like you're making sacrifices. In fact, embracing a frugal lifestyle can be a fun and rewarding way to take control of your finances, reduce stress, and achieve your long-term goals. By making small, practical changes to your spending habits, you can start saving money and enjoying the benefits of frugal living today.

One of the easiest and most effective ways to cut costs is to become a savvy shopper. Couponing, for example, can be a great way to save money on your regular purchases. Start by collecting coupons from newspapers, magazines, and online sources, and organize them in a way that makes sense for you. When you're ready to shop, take a few minutes to match your coupons with the items on your list, and watch the savings add up.

If you enjoy the thrill of the hunt, couponing can even become a fun hobby. You might join online forums or social media groups dedicated to couponing, where you can share tips, learn about the best deals, and celebrate your savings victories with like-minded individuals.

Another smart shopping strategy is price-matching. Many stores, especially larger retailers and grocery chains, will match the prices of their competitors. Before you head out to shop, take a few minutes to browse the weekly ads and circulars from other stores in your area. If you find a lower price on an item you need, bring the ad with you and ask the store to match the price. This simple step can save you money without requiring any extra time or effort on your part.

Price comparison apps and websites can also be valuable tools in your frugal living arsenal. These resources allow you to quickly and easily compare prices on everything from groceries and household essentials to clothing and electronics. By taking a moment to check prices before you buy, you can ensure that you're always getting the best deal possible.

Another way to embrace frugality is to get creative with your entertainment and leisure activities. Instead of spending money on expensive outings or subscriptions, look for free or low-cost alternatives that still allow you to have fun and enjoy your free time.

For example, instead of going to the movies or paying for a streaming service, check out free movies and TV shows from your local library. Many libraries also offer a wide range of free events and activities, like book clubs, craft workshops, and educational seminars, which can be a great way to learn new skills and meet like-minded people in your community.

If you enjoy staying active, look for free or low-cost ways to exercise and stay fit. Take advantage of public parks and trails for hiking, biking, or jogging, or check out free fitness classes and events in your area. You might also consider starting a walking or workout group with friends or neighbors, which can be a fun and social way to stay motivated and accountable.

When it comes to dining out, frugal living doesn't mean you have to give up your favorite restaurants or takeout meals entirely. Instead, look for ways to save money while still enjoying the occasional treat. Many restaurants offer daily specials, happy hour discounts, or loyalty programs that can help you save money on your bill. You might also consider splitting an entree with a friend or family member, or opting for appetizers or small plates instead of full meals.

At home, cooking your own meals can be a great way to save money and eat healthier. Plan your meals in advance, and make a grocery list based on the ingredients you'll need. Look for recipes that use inexpensive, versatile ingredients like rice, beans, and seasonal produce, and don't be afraid to get creative with leftovers or pantry staples.

Embracing frugal living can also be an opportunity to learn new skills and discover hidden talents. Consider learning how to sew, knit, or mend your own clothes, which can save you money on clothing repairs and alterations. If you're handy around the house, tackle minor home repairs and improvements yourself instead of hiring a professional. You might also consider starting a garden or learning how to preserve your own food, which can be a fun and rewarding way to save money on groceries.

Remember, frugal living is all about making small, sustainable changes that add up over time. Don't try to overhaul your entire lifestyle overnight - instead, focus on one or two changes at a time, and gradually build on your success. Celebrate your savings victories, no matter how small, and use them as motivation to keep going.

As you embrace frugality, you might be surprised at how much fun and fulfillment you can find in a simpler, more intentional way of life. By cutting costs and focusing on the things that truly matter to you, you'll not only save money, but also reduce stress, improve your financial security, and create more space in your life for the people and experiences that bring you joy.

In the next section, we'll dive deeper into the world of frugal meal planning and cooking, exploring practical strategies for saving money on groceries and eating well on a budget. From meal prep and batch cooking to using leftovers and shopping in season, you'll learn how to eat healthily and deliciously without breaking the bank.

MEAL PLANNING AND LIFESTYLE TWEAKS

Meal planning, bulk buying, and DIY home projects are three powerful strategies for cutting expenses and living more frugally without sacrificing quality or enjoyment. By taking a creative, solution-focused approach to these areas of your life, you can significantly reduce your spending, minimize waste, and create a more intentional, fulfilling lifestyle.

Let's start by exploring the benefits of meal planning. At its core, meal planning is about being proactive and strategic with your food choices. Instead of deciding what to eat on a day-to-day basis, which can often lead to impulse purchases, wasted ingredients, and less healthy choices, meal planning involves thinking ahead and creating a structured plan for your meals and snacks.

To get started with meal planning, set aside some time each week to plan out your meals for the upcoming days. Consider your schedule, dietary preferences, and any upcoming events or special occasions. Look for recipes that use similar ingredients, so you can maximize your grocery purchases and minimize waste.

For example, if you're planning to make a chicken stir-fry one night, you might also plan to use the leftover chicken in a soup or salad later in the week. By being strategic with your ingredient choices, you can stretch your grocery budget further and ensure that nothing goes to waste.

As you plan your meals, also consider how you can incorporate bulk buying into your shopping strategy. Buying in bulk can be a great way to save money on the items you use most frequently, like grains, legumes, nuts, and seeds.

When you buy these items in larger quantities, you often pay a lower price per unit than you would if you bought them in smaller packages. Plus, by having a well-stocked pantry, you'll be better equipped to whip up healthy, delicious meals at a moment's notice, without having to run to the store for last-minute ingredients.

When bulk buying, be sure to consider your storage space and the shelf life of the items you're purchasing. Opt for ingredients that have a long shelf life and that you know you'll use regularly to avoid waste. You might also consider splitting bulk purchases with a friend or family member to save money and ensure that you're able to use everything before it expires.

Another area where you can significantly reduce expenses is through DIY home projects. From home repairs and renovations to simple decor updates, taking a DIY approach can save you hundreds or even thousands of dollars compared to hiring professionals.

Start by assessing your skills and interests. If you enjoy working with your hands and have some basic tools and knowledge, you might be surprised at how many projects you can tackle on your own.

For example, painting a room, updating hardware on cabinets, or even installing a new light fixture are all relatively simple projects that can make a big impact on the look and feel of your home, without breaking the bank.

As you take on DIY projects, remember to approach them with a creative, solution-focused mindset. If you encounter a challenge or roadblock, don't get discouraged. Instead, see it as an opportunity to learn and grow. Look for resources like online tutorials, how-to books, or community workshops that can help you expand your skills and knowledge.

You might also consider joining a local DIY group or online forum, where you can connect with other like-minded individuals and share tips, techniques, and inspiration. By surrounding yourself with a supportive community of fellow DIYers, you'll be more motivated to take on new projects and push yourself creatively.

When tackling DIY projects, it's also important to know your limits and to prioritize safety. If a project feels too complex or risky, or if it requires specialized tools or knowledge that you don't have, it may be worth investing in professional help. Remember, the goal of frugal living isn't to cut corners or take unnecessary risks, but rather to be thoughtful and strategic with your resources.

Ultimately, by embracing meal planning, bulk buying, and DIY home projects, you can significantly reduce your expenses and create a more intentional, fulfilling lifestyle. These strategies not only save you money, but also empower you to take control of your choices, minimize waste, and create a home and life that truly reflects your values and priorities.

As you incorporate these frugal living strategies into your daily routines, remember to approach them with a spirit of creativity, curiosity, and fun. See meal planning as an opportunity to experiment with new recipes and flavors, bulk buying as a chance to stock your pantry with wholesome, nourishing ingredients, and DIY projects as a way to express your unique style and vision.

By embracing a solution-focused mindset and being open to learning and growth, you'll not only reduce your expenses, but also cultivate a deeper sense of self-sufficiency, resilience, and joy in your daily life.

So go ahead and give these strategies a try - start small, be patient with yourself, and celebrate your progress along the way. As you begin to see the benefits of frugal living firsthand, you'll be inspired to keep exploring new ways to save money, live more intentionally, and create a life that truly aligns with your values and goals.

In the next section, we'll explore the power of mindset shifts in creating sustainable, long-term changes in your financial habits and overall quality of life. From reframing the concept of "sacrifice" to cultivating gratitude and contentment, you'll learn how small shifts in your thinking can lead to big transformations in your financial and personal well-being.

Mindset Shifts for Sustainable Saving

When it comes to living frugally and saving money, one of the most powerful tools at your disposal is your mindset. By reframing the way you think about spending, saving, and your overall relationship with money, you can create sustainable, long-lasting changes in your financial habits and overall quality of life.

At the heart of this mindset shift is the idea of reframing "sacrifice" as an "investment in the future." Often, when we think about cutting expenses or living on a budget, we focus on what we're giving up in the present moment. We might feel like we're sacrificing our comfort, convenience, or enjoyment for the sake of saving money.

However, what if we flipped this script and instead focused on what we're gaining in the long run? Every dollar you save, every expense you cut, every frugal choice you make - these aren't sacrifices, but rather investments in your future self and the life you want to create.

Think of it like planting a garden. When you plant a seed, you're not sacrificing the seed itself, but rather investing it in the potential for growth and abundance. You're putting in the time, effort, and resources now, knowing that in the future, you'll reap the rewards of a bountiful harvest.

The same principle applies to your finances. When you choose to cook a meal at home instead of eating out, you're not sacrificing the experience of dining out, but rather investing in your health, your savings, and your long-term financial security. When you choose to buy a used car instead of a brand new one, you're not sacrificing luxury or status, but rather investing in your freedom from debt and the peace of mind that comes with owning your vehicle outright.

By reframing your thinking in this way, you can shift your focus from what you're giving up to what you're gaining. You can start to see frugal living not as a burden or a chore, but as a powerful tool for creating the life you want to live.

Of course, making this mindset shift isn't always easy, especially if you're used to a certain way of thinking about money and spending. That's why it's important to approach frugal living with a sense of curiosity, experimentation, and self-compassion.

Start by setting small, achievable goals for yourself. Maybe you want to save an extra $50 per month, or cut your dining out expenses by half. Whatever your goal, break it down into smaller, manageable steps and celebrate your progress along the way.

As you work towards your goals, be patient with yourself and remember that change takes time. There may be setbacks or moments of frustration, but these are all opportunities for learning and growth. Instead of beating yourself up for a slip-up or a moment of weakness, use it as a chance to reflect on what you can do differently next time, and recommit to your goals with renewed focus and determination.

Another key to maintaining a sense of fulfillment while living on a budget is to focus on the things that truly matter to you. Often, when we're used to a certain way of spending, we can lose sight of what really brings us joy and satisfaction in life.

Take some time to reflect on your values, your passions, and the things that make you feel truly alive. Maybe it's spending time with loved ones, pursuing a creative hobby, or exploring the great outdoors. Whatever it is, make sure to prioritize these things in your life, even as you work towards your financial goals.

Remember, frugal living isn't about deprivation or sacrifice, but rather about being intentional and mindful with your resources. It's about aligning your spending with your values and your long-term vision for your life.

So as you embrace this mindset shift and start to see the benefits of frugal living firsthand, remember to approach the process with a spirit of openness, curiosity, and self-compassion. Surround yourself with supportive, like-minded people who share your values and can encourage you along the way.

And above all, keep your eye on the prize - the life of financial freedom, security, and abundance that you're working so hard to create. Every frugal choice you make, every dollar you save, every investment you make in your future self - these are all steps on the path to creating a life that truly aligns with your deepest values and aspirations.

So go forth with confidence, knowing that by shifting your mindset and embracing the power of frugal living, you're not just changing your financial habits, but transforming your entire perspective on what it means to live a rich, fulfilling life. The rewards of this journey are truly limitless, and they're waiting for you to claim them, one small, intentional choice at a time.

In the next chapter, we'll dive into the world of beginner-friendly investing, exploring how even small, consistent investments in low-risk vehicles like savings accounts, CDs, and index funds can help you grow your wealth and secure your financial future over the long term. Get ready to take your frugal living journey to the next level!

SMART SPENDING, HAPPY LIVING

Throughout our exploration of budgeting strategies, we've seen how mindful money management can provide a solid foundation for financial wellbeing. But as we delve deeper into the nuances of personal finance, it's important to acknowledge that true prosperity goes beyond the numbers in our bank accounts. Financial success is not just about accumulating wealth; it's about using our resources in a way that aligns with our values, supports our goals, and enhances our overall quality of life.

In the previous chapter, we focused on the vital role of savings in building a robust financial safety net. We discussed strategies for effortlessly growing your emergency fund, such as automating transfers and harnessing the power of incremental progress. These habits lay the groundwork for weathering life's unexpected challenges with greater ease and resilience.

But saving is just one side of the financial wellness equation. To truly thrive, it's equally important to develop a healthy, purposeful approach to spending. That's where the concepts of frugality and intentional living come into play.

Frugality, at its core, is about being resourceful and mindful with your money. It's not about deprivation or sacrifice, but rather about making conscious choices that prioritize your long-term financial health and personal fulfillment. By embracing frugal habits like smart shopping, DIY projects, and creative problem-solving, you can stretch your resources further without compromising your quality of life.

Throughout this chapter, we've explored practical strategies for integrating frugality into your daily routines. From simple life hacks like meal planning and energy conservation to bigger-picture shifts like embracing minimalism and valuing experiences over possessions, these techniques can help you spend more intentionally and in alignment with your deepest values.

We've also delved into the psychological dimensions of frugal living, discussing the importance of cultivating an abundance mindset and finding contentment in the present moment. By reframing frugality as a path to greater freedom, creativity, and purpose, you can transform your relationship with money from one of stress and scarcity to one of empowerment and opportunity.

Ultimately, the goal of smart spending isn't just to save money for its own sake, but to create a life that is rich in the things that matter most to you. Whether that means investing in experiences that bring you joy, supporting causes you believe in, or building a financial legacy for your loved ones, mindful money management is a tool for crafting a life of purpose and fulfillment.

As we've seen through real-life examples and success stories, frugal living is a skill that anyone can learn with practice and persistence. By starting small, celebrating your progress, and staying open to new ideas and strategies, you can gradually transform your spending habits in a way that feels sustainable and empowering.

Of course, smart spending is just one piece of the larger financial puzzle. To truly harness the power of your money, it's also important to develop a basic understanding of investing principles. In the next chapter, we'll explore beginner-friendly investment pathways like savings accounts, CDs, and index funds, discussing how these tools can help you grow your wealth steadily and sustainably over time. By combining frugal habits with a long-term investment strategy, you'll be well-equipped to navigate your financial journey with confidence and clarity.

CHAPTER EIGHT

BEGINNER-FRIENDLY INVESTMENT PATHWAYS

When you're just starting out on your investing journey, the sheer number of options can feel overwhelming. Stocks, bonds, mutual funds, ETFs - it's a lot to take in, especially if you're new to the world of finance. But here's the good news: you don't need to be an expert to start investing wisely. In fact, some of the best investment strategies for beginners are also the simplest.

In this chapter, we'll explore three beginner-friendly investment pathways that can help you start growing your wealth without taking on too much risk. We'll start with low-risk savings vehicles like traditional savings accounts and Certificates of Deposit (CDs). These may not offer the highest returns, but they're a great place to park your emergency fund or any money you might need in the short term.

Next, we'll dive into the world of index funds. These handy investment tools allow you to instantly diversify your portfolio across hundreds of stocks or bonds, without having to pick individual companies yourself. By simply tracking a market index, index funds offer an easy, low-cost way to start building long-term wealth.

Finally, we'll discuss how to know when you're ready to level up your investment game. As you become more comfortable with the basics and your financial situation evolves, you may want to start exploring more advanced strategies, like diversifying into real estate, branching out into sector-specific funds, or even dabbling in individual stocks.

The key is to take things one step at a time and always keep learning. Investing is a lifelong journey, and even the most successful investors started somewhere. By focusing on simple, proven strategies and making regular contributions over time, you can harness the power of compound growth and watch your nest egg steadily rise.

Remember, investing is not about getting rich quick - it's about making smart, disciplined choices that align with your goals and risk tolerance. With the beginner-friendly pathways outlined in this chapter, you'll be well on your way to building a solid financial foundation and creating long-term wealth.

So take a deep breath, grab a notebook, and let's dive in. Your investing adventure starts now, and we're excited to be your guide along the way.

In the first section, we'll take a closer look at low-risk savings accounts and CDs. These may not be the flashiest investment vehicles, but they play a crucial role in any well-rounded financial plan. Let's explore how these simple savings tools can help you build a strong foundation for your investing future.

LOW-RISK SAVINGS AND CDs

When you're just starting your financial journey, it's natural to feel a bit overwhelmed by all the different investment options out there. But don't worry—you don't have to dive into the deep end right away. In fact, one of the smartest moves you can make as a beginner is to focus on low-risk savings vehicles like traditional savings accounts and Certificates of Deposit (CDs).

Let's start with savings accounts. You're probably already familiar with these — they're the basic accounts offered by banks and credit unions where you can safely store your money and earn a little bit of interest in return. The biggest advantage of savings accounts is that they're incredibly low-risk. In most cases, your deposits are insured by the Federal Deposit Insurance Corporation (FDIC) for up to $250,000, meaning you won't lose your money even if the bank goes under.

The downside? Savings accounts typically offer pretty low interest rates, often less than 1% annual percentage yield (APY). That means your money will grow slowly over time. However, savings accounts are still a great place to park your emergency fund or any cash you might need in the short term, like saving up for a down payment on a car or a holiday gift budget.

Now, let's talk about Certificates of Deposit, or CDs. These are a bit like savings accounts with a twist. With a CD, you agree to leave your money in the account for a set period of time—usually anywhere from a few months to a few years. In exchange, the bank offers you a higher interest rate than you'd get with a standard savings account.

The catch? You typically can't withdraw your money from a CD before the end of the term without paying a penalty. That means CDs are best for funds you know you won't need for a while, like a portion of your emergency savings or money you're setting aside for a longer-term goal like a down payment on a house.

So, how do savings accounts and CDs fit into your overall financial plan as a beginner? Think of them as the foundation of your savings strategy. Before you start investing in the stock market or exploring other higher-risk options, it's a good idea to have a solid base of savings that you can easily access if you need to.

A smart approach is to set up a regular savings account for your emergency fund—aim to save enough to cover three to six months' worth of living expenses. Then, consider putting any additional savings into CDs with varying term lengths (this is called "laddering"). That way, you'll always have some CDs maturing and available if you need the cash, while the rest of your money keeps earning those higher interest rates.

Remember, building your savings is a marathon, not a sprint. By starting with low-risk options like savings accounts and CDs, you're laying a strong foundation for your financial future. As your knowledge and confidence grow, you can start exploring more advanced investment strategies to help your money work even harder for you. But for now, focus on establishing those good savings habits and watching your nest egg steadily grow.

In the next section, we'll take a closer look at another beginner-friendly investment option: index funds. These offer a simple way to start investing in the stock market without the risks of picking individual stocks. Get ready to learn how index funds can help you build long-term wealth!

Index Funds 101

Picture this: you're at a carnival, and you're eyeing the prizes at the ring toss booth. You could try to win the giant stuffed panda by landing a ring on a single bottle—but that's pretty risky. Your chances of winning are slim, and you might walk away empty-handed. But what if there was a way to win a bunch of smaller prizes by spreading your rings across all the bottles? That's kind of like how index funds work in investing.

An index fund is a type of mutual fund or exchange-traded fund (ETF) that aims to match the performance of a specific market index, like the S&P 500. Instead of trying to beat the market by picking individual stocks, index funds simply try to be the market.

Here's how it works: an index fund holds a diverse collection of stocks or bonds—sometimes hundreds or even thousands—in proportions that mirror a particular index. For example, an S&P 500 index fund would invest in all 500 companies in that index, in the same proportions as the index itself.

Why is this a less risky approach than buying individual stocks? Well, think back to our carnival analogy. When you buy an individual stock, you're betting on the success of a single company. If that company hits a rough patch or even goes bankrupt, your investment could take a hefty hit. But when you invest in an index fund, you're spreading your money across a wide range of companies. Sure, some of those companies might underperform, but others will likely outperform—and the overall diversity helps balance out the risk.

In fact, studies have shown that over the long term, index funds often outperform actively managed funds, where professional investors try to hand-pick winning stocks. Why? Because index funds typically have much lower fees than actively managed funds. Those fees can really eat into your returns over time.

So, how do you get started with index funds? The first step is to choose a broad market index that aligns with your investment goals. For many beginners, an S&P 500 index fund is a good place to start, since it offers exposure to a wide swath of the U.S. stock market. But there are index funds for just about every market segment you can think of—from bonds to international stocks to real estate.

Once you've chosen an index, you can invest in an index fund through a brokerage account or directly through a mutual fund company. Many employers also offer index fund options in their 401(k) plans.

One key thing to remember: index funds are designed to be long-term investments. They're not about making a quick buck; they're about harnessing the power of the market over time. That means you shouldn't invest money you might need in the short term, like next month's rent or your emergency fund. Instead, consider index funds for goals that are at least five years away, like saving for a down payment on a house or building your retirement nest egg.

Now, all this isn't to say that index funds are completely risk-free—no investment is. When the overall market goes down, index funds will follow suit. But for most investors, particularly beginners, the broad diversification and low costs of index funds make them a smart way to start building wealth in the stock market.

As you learn more about investing and become more comfortable with risk, you may want to start exploring more specialized index funds or even dipping a toe into individual stocks. But for now, think of index funds as your trusty carnival companion—they may not win you the biggest prize, but they'll help you walk away with a bunch of smaller ones, and that can really add up over time!

The key is to start investing as early as you can, even if it's just a little bit each month. With the power of compound returns, time is your greatest ally in investing. And index funds make it easy to harness that power, even as a beginner.

Stay tuned for our next section, where we'll explore how to know when you're ready to level up your investment game. We'll discuss signs that you're ready to take on a bit more risk and strategies for diversifying your portfolio as your wealth grows.

When and How to Level Up Your Investments

As you've started to get comfortable with basic investment vehicles like savings accounts, CDs, and index funds, you might be wondering: when is it time to take the next step? When should you start diversifying your portfolio and exploring more advanced investment strategies?

The truth is, there's no one-size-fits-all answer. The right time to level up your investments depends on a variety of factors, including your financial goals, your risk tolerance, your time horizon, and your overall financial stability.

One key indicator that you might be ready to diversify is if you've built up a solid emergency fund and paid off any high-interest debt, like credit card balances. These financial foundational blocks should always come first, before you start thinking about more complex investments.

Another sign that you might be ready to expand your investment horizons is if you've gotten comfortable with the basics of investing and you're eager to learn more. Maybe you've been reading up on different types of investments, like bonds, REITs (real estate investment trusts), or ETFs (exchange-traded funds). Or perhaps you've been following the financial news and have a better understanding of how market conditions can impact different sectors and asset classes.

If you're nodding your head to these indicators, then it might be time to start thinking about diversifying your portfolio. But what does that actually mean?

In simple terms, diversification is about spreading your investment risk across different types of assets. The idea is that if one part of your portfolio takes a hit (like if the stock market dips), other parts of your portfolio might remain stable or even rise in value (like bonds, which often move in the opposite direction of stocks).

Think of it like a balanced meal. If you only eat pizza every day, you might get sick of it pretty quickly (and it's not very good for you). But if you eat a variety of foods—some fruits, some veggies, some grains, some protein—you'll get a wider range of nutrients and likely feel more satisfied overall. Your investment portfolio works the same way.

So, how do you actually go about diversifying? A good place to start is by looking at your current allocation between stocks and bonds. As a general rule of thumb, the younger you are, the more you can afford to be weighted towards stocks, which tend to be riskier but also offer higher potential returns over the long term. As you get closer to retirement age, you might want to start shifting more of your portfolio into bonds, which offer more stability and income.

You can also diversify within asset classes. For example, instead of just investing in an S&P 500 index fund, you might also consider index funds that focus on smaller companies, international stocks, or specific sectors like technology or healthcare.

Another way to diversify is through alternative investments, like real estate, commodities, or even cryptocurrency. These can be more complex and often require more research and due diligence, but they can also offer the potential for higher returns and help hedge against inflation and market volatility.

The key is to start slowly and educate yourself as you go. Don't feel like you need to jump into complex investment strategies right away. Even simple steps, like adding a bond index fund to your portfolio or opening a Roth IRA for retirement savings, can help you start to diversify.

There are also plenty of resources available to help guide you as you level up your investments. Consider reading books on investing, subscribing to financial newsletters or podcasts, or even working with a financial advisor who can help you create a personalized investment plan.

Remember, investing is a lifelong journey. As your financial situation changes — maybe you get a raise, or you have a child, or you start thinking about retiring early — your investment strategy will likely need to change too. The key is to stay informed, stay engaged, and stay focused on your long-term goals.

By taking small steps to diversify your portfolio over time, you can gradually level up your investment game and work towards building long-term wealth and financial security. And don't be afraid to ask for help along the way — whether it's from a trusted financial professional or just by bouncing ideas off a savvy friend or family member.

The most important thing is to keep learning, keep growing, and keep taking action towards your financial dreams. With time, patience, and a willingness to step outside your comfort zone, you can become a confident, diversified investor — and reap the rewards for years to come.

Speaking of taking action, in our next chapter, we'll explore the importance of regularly tracking, reviewing, and adjusting your budget. Just like with investing, your budget is a living, breathing thing that will change as your life changes. By staying on top of it and making small tweaks along the way, you can ensure that you're always making progress towards your financial goals. Let's dive in!

Planting Seeds for Future Wealth

As we've journeyed through the landscape of personal finance, we've discovered that the path to lasting prosperity is paved with small, consistent actions. From crafting a budget that aligns with our values to cultivating a mindset of frugality and purpose, each deliberate choice we make with our money is like planting a tiny seed—a seed that, with time, care, and nurturing, can blossom into a bountiful harvest of financial security and abundance.

In the previous chapter, we delved into the transformative power of consciously directing our spending towards what matters most. By learning to differentiate between "needs" and "wants," practicing gratitude for what we already have, and finding creative ways to stretch our resources, we can experience a profound sense of contentment and fulfillment, even as we work towards our larger financial goals.

But as important as mindful spending is, it's only one piece of the wealth-building puzzle. To truly set ourselves up for long-term financial success, it's crucial to also develop the habit of consistent, strategic investing.

At first glance, the world of investing can seem intimidating, especially for those just starting out. With so many options, from stocks and bonds to real estate and cryptocurrencies, it's easy to feel overwhelmed and unsure of where to begin. However, as we've explored throughout this chapter, getting started with investing doesn't have to be complicated or require vast sums of money. In fact, some of the most effective investment strategies are also the simplest.

One key insight we've gleaned is the power of beginning with low-risk, low-complexity investment vehicles, such as high-yield savings accounts and Certificates of Deposit (CDs). While these options may not offer the highest potential returns, they provide a stable, secure foundation upon which to build our investment journey. By parking our short-term savings or emergency fund in these FDIC-insured accounts, we can earn a modest return while ensuring our money is safe and easily accessible when we need it.

As our knowledge and confidence grow, we can start to explore more growth-oriented investment options, such as index funds. These handy tools allow us to instantly diversify our portfolios across hundreds of stocks or bonds, without the need to painstakingly research and select individual companies. By simply tracking a broad market index, like the S&P 500, we can harness the power of the market's overall growth while minimizing the risks of individual stock picking.

Throughout our exploration of beginner-friendly investment strategies, a few key principles have emerged:

1. Start early and invest consistently. Thanks to the magic of compound interest, even small contributions can snowball into significant wealth over time. The earlier we begin investing, the more time our money has to grow.

2. Diversify our investments to manage risk. By spreading our money across different asset classes, sectors, and geographies, we can create a more balanced, resilient portfolio that weathers market ups and downs.

3. Keep fees and costs low. Over time, even seemingly small management fees and transaction costs can take a big bite out of our investment returns. By favoring low-cost index funds over actively managed ones, we can keep more of our money working for us.

4. Stay patient and think long-term. Building wealth through investing is a marathon, not a sprint. By staying focused on our long-term goals and avoiding the temptation to constantly tinker with our portfolios, we can ride out short-term market volatility and give our investments the time they need to compound and grow.

Of course, these principles are just a starting point. As we continue on our financial learning journey, we may choose to explore more advanced investment strategies, such as value investing, real estate investing, or dividend growth investing. The key is to build a strong foundation of knowledge and begin taking action, even if it feels small at first.

By combining the power of intentional spending with the long-term growth potential of consistent investing, we can gradually transform our financial lives from a state of scarcity and stress to one of abundance and possibility. Each dollar we mindfully save or wisely invest is like a tiny seed, packed with the potential to sprout, grow, and bear fruit over time.

As we move forward on this journey of financial empowerment, we must remember that our money is ultimately a tool—a tool for crafting a life of purpose, joy, and generosity. By aligning our financial choices with our deepest values and continually expanding our knowledge and skills, we can harness the power of our resources to not only secure our own futures, but also to make a positive impact on the world around us.

In the next chapter, we'll explore the importance of regularly reviewing and adjusting our budgets and financial plans. Just as a well-tended garden requires ongoing care and attention, our financial lives thrive with consistent monitoring, pruning, and adaptation. By learning to embrace the ebbs and flows of our financial journeys with flexibility and grace, we can stay rooted in our values while continuing to grow and flourish over time.

CHAPTER NINE

TRACKING, REVIEWING, AND ADJUSTING YOUR BUDGET

Congratulations on making it this far in your budgeting journey! By now, you've learned how to set up a budget that aligns with your unique goals and values, and you've started putting those skills into practice in your daily life. But as any experienced budgeter will tell you, creating a budget is only the beginning. To truly harness the power of budgeting as a tool for financial transformation, you need to make it a regular, ongoing practice.

That's where tracking, reviewing, and adjusting come in. In this chapter, we'll explore the importance of checking in on your budget regularly, both to celebrate your progress and to identify areas for improvement. We'll discuss different review cycles and cadences you might consider, from monthly check-ins to annual assessments, and provide tips for making these reviews as productive and painless as possible.

But we'll also acknowledge an important truth: life is full of unexpected twists and turns, and even the most carefully crafted budget will need to adapt and evolve over time. That's why we'll delve into the concept of flexibility and discuss strategies for pivoting your budget when your circumstances change. Whether you're facing a job loss, a growing family, or a sudden windfall, we'll show you how to approach these transitions with a spirit of resilience and adaptability.

Throughout the chapter, we'll bring these concepts to life with real-world examples and success stories. You'll meet individuals and families who have used budgeting to weather financial storms, achieve big dreams, and transform their relationships with money. These stories will inspire you and remind you that budgeting is a powerful tool that can work for anyone, no matter their starting point or challenges.

As you read, remember that budgeting is a deeply personal practice. What works for one person may not work for another, and that's okay. The key is to find a rhythm and approach that feels sustainable and empowering for you. By staying engaged with your budget, remaining open to change, and celebrating your progress along the way, you'll be well on your way to lasting financial success.

So grab your favorite beverage, settle in, and let's dive into the world of tracking, reviewing, and adjusting your budget. Your future self will thank you for the investment you're making today.

In the first section, we'll take a closer look at review cycles and check-ins. We'll explore why regular budget reviews are so important, and provide some tips for making them a consistent, stress-free part of your financial routine. Get ready to take your budgeting skills to the next level!

Review Cycles and Check-Ins

Just like how regular check-ups with your doctor help you stay physically healthy, frequent budget reviews are key to maintaining robust financial health. But how often should you be checking in on your budget, and what should you be looking for during these financial self-exams? Let's break it down.

For most people, a monthly budget review is a good cadence to start with. Think of it as a standing appointment with yourself, a sacred time carved out to focus on your financial wellbeing. Mark it on your calendar, set a reminder on your phone, do whatever it takes to make this budget review a non-negotiable part of your routine.

During these monthly check-ins, your main goal is to compare your actual spending and saving against the budget plan you set for yourself. It's like holding a mirror up to your financial life—an opportunity to honestly assess what's working well and what might need some adjusting.

One of the key indicators to look at is your income versus your expenses. Are you bringing in as much money as you expected this month? Did any unexpected windfalls or shortfalls occur? On the expense side, did you stick to your planned spending in each category, or were there areas where you went over budget?

Don't worry if the numbers don't always match up perfectly with your plan — that's normal, especially when you're first starting to budget. The important thing is to understand why any discrepancies occurred and to make a game plan for addressing them going forward.

For example, let's say you budgeted $300 for groceries this month, but you ended up spending $400. During your budget review, take some time to reflect on what happened. Did you host an unexpected dinner party or buy more expensive ingredients than usual? Did you succumb to impulse buys at the checkout counter? Once you identify the root cause, you can come up with a strategy to prevent overspending next month, whether that's planning your meals more carefully, shopping with a list, or avoiding temptation by ordering groceries online.

Another key indicator to check is your progress towards your financial goals. Are you managing to set aside the amount you planned for your emergency fund, your retirement account, your down payment savings? If not, what obstacles got in the way, and how can you course-correct for next month?

Celebrating your wins is just as important as identifying areas for improvement. Did you successfully stick to your entertainment budget this month, even though there were a lot of tempting concerts and events happening? Did you make an extra payment towards your student loans? Take a moment to pat yourself on the back and recognize these milestones, no matter how small. Positive reinforcement can be a powerful motivator to keep you engaged with your budget for the long haul.

Now, while a monthly budget review is a great baseline, there may be times when you want to check in more frequently. If you're working towards a particularly challenging financial goal, like paying off a large credit card balance, you might benefit from weekly or even daily check-ins to keep yourself accountable and on track.

On the flip side, once you've gotten the hang of budgeting and feel confident in your ability to manage your money, you might decide to space out your formal reviews to once a quarter. The key is to find a rhythm that works for you and your lifestyle, one that keeps you engaged and informed without feeling like a burdensome chore.

Regardless of how often you conduct your formal budget reviews, it's important to stay mindful of your spending and saving on a day-to-day basis. This is where tracking tools like budgeting apps or even a simple spreadsheet can come in handy. By inputting your transactions in real-time (or at least every few days), you can keep a pulse on your financial progress and quickly spot any potential issues before they snowball into bigger problems.

The goal of all this tracking and reviewing isn't to make you feel restricted or beholden to your budget. Rather, it's to empower you with the knowledge and awareness you need to make informed choices about your money. The more in tune you are with your financial situation, the more confident you'll feel in your ability to navigate life's inevitable ups and downs.

Remember, budgeting is a skill, and like any skill, it takes practice to master. Be patient with yourself, celebrate your progress, and don't be afraid to make adjustments as you go. With each budget review, you're taking a proactive step towards your financial dreams, and that's something to be proud of.

In the next section, we'll explore the importance of embracing flexibility in your budget. Life has a way of throwing curveballs at us, and sometimes our financial plans need to shift in response. By building adaptability into your budgeting mindset from the start, you'll be better equipped to handle whatever comes your way.

EMBRACING FLEXIBILITY

One of the most important things to remember about budgeting is that it's not a set-it-and-forget-it kind of thing. Your budget is a living, breathing document that should evolve and change as your life does. And that's not just okay — it's actually a sign that you're doing it right!

Think about it: would you expect a single pair of shoes to fit you perfectly from childhood all the way through adulthood? Of course not! As you grow and change, your shoes need to change with you. The same is true for your budget.

Throughout your life, you'll experience all sorts of shifts and transitions that can impact your financial situation. Maybe you'll land a new job with a higher salary, or maybe you'll decide to go back to school and pursue a new career path. Maybe you'll get married, have children, or move to a new city with a different cost of living. All of these life changes come with their own set of financial implications, and your budget will need to adapt accordingly.

So, how can you pivot your budget without feeling like you've failed or gotten off track? The first step is to reframe your mindset around budgeting altogether. Instead of viewing your budget as a rigid set of rules that you have to follow perfectly, try to think of it as a flexible framework that's designed to support you and your evolving needs.

When a major life change occurs, take a step back and reassess your financial landscape. What new expenses do you need to account for? What income streams might be impacted? What goals and priorities might need to shift?

For example, let's say you and your partner decide to start a family. Suddenly, you're facing a whole new set of expenses—diapers, childcare, possibly a larger living space. At the same time, one of you might choose to step back from work to be a full-time parent, reducing your household income.

In this scenario, it's not only okay to modify your budget—it's absolutely necessary! You'll need to recalibrate your spending categories to accommodate your new reality, perhaps allocating more money towards things like groceries and healthcare while scaling back on discretionary expenses like travel or entertainment.

The key is to approach these changes with a spirit of flexibility and self-compassion. Remember, the goal of budgeting isn't to adhere to some arbitrary set of rules—it's to create a spending and saving plan that aligns with your unique values, goals, and circumstances.

If you find yourself struggling to adapt your budget to a new situation, don't be afraid to seek out help and guidance. Talk to your partner or a trusted friend about your concerns, or consider working with a financial coach or advisor who can offer expert insights and strategies.

Another helpful tip is to build some wiggle room into your budget from the start. When you're setting up your initial spending categories and allocations, try to leave a little bit of breathing room in each area. That way, when unexpected expenses pop up or your circumstances change, you'll have some built-in flexibility to work with.

It's also important to remember that pivoting your budget isn't a one-time event. As your life continues to unfold and evolve, your budget will need to do the same. That's why those regular budget reviews and check-ins we discussed earlier are so important—they give you a structured opportunity to step back, reassess, and make any necessary adjustments.

The bottom line? Embracing flexibility in your budget isn't a sign of failure—it's a sign of financial resilience and adaptability. By allowing your budget to bend and flex with the contours of your life, you're setting yourself up for long-term success and peace of mind.

So the next time you face a major life transition or unexpected curveball, remember: it's not about rigidly sticking to a pre-determined plan. It's about having the courage and wisdom to pivot when necessary, and to keep steering your financial ship towards the horizons that matter most to you.

And speaking of staying the course, that's exactly what we'll be discussing in the next section. We'll explore some real-life examples and success stories of people who've navigated their own budget pivots and come out stronger on the other side. Get ready to be inspired!

REAL-LIFE EXAMPLES AND SUCCESS STORIES

Throughout this book, we've explored the ins and outs of budgeting—from setting up your first spending plan to navigating the inevitable twists and turns that life throws your way. But what does this process actually look like in practice? How have real people used budgeting to transform their financial lives and achieve their dreams?

Let's dive into a few inspiring examples.

Meet Jessica, a 28-year-old marketing professional living in Chicago. When Jessica first started budgeting, she was saddled with over $25,000 in student loan debt and had very little savings to her name. She felt overwhelmed and discouraged, unsure of how she would ever get ahead.

But then Jessica decided to take control. She sat down and created a detailed budget, mapping out her income and expenses and identifying areas where she could cut back. She started cooking more meals at home, shopping for groceries with a list, and saying no to pricey nights out with friends.

At the same time, Jessica looked for ways to boost her income. She took on a few freelance projects in her spare time and negotiated a raise at her day job. Little by little, she started chipping away at her debt while also building up her emergency fund.

Fast forward two years, and Jessica's financial picture looks very different. She's paid off all but $5,000 of her student loans, has a robust emergency fund that could cover six months of expenses, and is starting to invest for her future. But perhaps most importantly, Jessica feels a sense of confidence and empowerment around her finances that she never had before.

"Budgeting completely changed my relationship with money," she says. "It helped me take control of my spending, prioritize what matters most to me, and make meaningful progress towards my goals. It wasn't always easy, but it was so worth it."

Jessica's story is a powerful reminder that budgeting isn't about perfection—it's about progress. Even small changes, made consistently over time, can add up to big results.

Or consider the example of Mark and Emily, a couple in their mid-30s who found themselves facing an unexpected budget pivot when Emily lost her job due to a company downsizing. Suddenly, they were down to one income and facing a lot of uncertainty about their financial future.

Rather than panicking or giving up on their budget altogether, Mark and Emily chose to adapt. They sat down together and took a hard look at their spending, identifying areas where they could temporarily cut back while Emily looked for a new job. They put their gym memberships on hold, switched to a cheaper cell phone plan, and started having more budget-friendly date nights at home.

At the same time, they made sure to communicate openly and honestly with each other about their fears and concerns. They leaned on their emergency fund to help cover their essential expenses, and Emily focused on networking and upskilling to make herself a more competitive job candidate.

It wasn't an easy time, but because Mark and Emily had a solid budgeting foundation in place, they were able to weather the storm. And when Emily did land a new job several months later, they were in a strong position to not only get back on track with their original budget but to start planning for some exciting new goals, like saving for a down payment on a house.

"Losing my job was scary, but having a budget in place gave us a roadmap to follow," Emily reflects. "It helped us stay focused on what mattered most and make smart choices with the resources we had. And now, we feel more prepared than ever to handle whatever challenges come our way."

Mark and Emily's experience highlights the power of flexibility and teamwork in budgeting. Life is full of ups and downs, but when you have a budgeting buddy by your side and a willingness to roll with the punches, you can overcome even the toughest of financial curveballs.

These are just two examples among countless others. From the single mom who used budgeting to save up for her dream home, to the recent college grad who paid off their loans in record time, to the empty nesters who used their newfound budget skills to travel the world, the possibilities are endless.

The common thread in all of these stories is a commitment to the budgeting process—not just as a one-time exercise, but as an ongoing practice of financial mindfulness and intentional living. These folks didn't just create a budget and then set it aside; they used it as a living, breathing tool to help them align their spending with their values and goals.

And here's the beautiful thing: this same power is available to you, too. No matter where you're starting from or what challenges you're facing, budgeting can be your key to unlocking a brighter financial future.

So as we wrap up this chapter and prepare to explore the long-term road ahead, take a moment to reflect on your own budgeting journey so far. What successes have you achieved, both big and small? What obstacles have you overcome? What lessons have you learned?

Most importantly, what dreams and goals are calling to you from the other side of your budgeting journey? Whether it's paying off debt, saving for a once-in-a-lifetime adventure, starting your own business, or simply building a life of greater security and peace of mind, your budget can help you get there—one purposeful step at a time.

In the next chapter, we'll explore some strategies for staying the course with your budget for the long haul. We'll talk about how to overcome plateaus and setbacks, how to keep learning and growing in your financial knowledge, and how to celebrate your wins along the way.

Because ultimately, budgeting isn't a sprint—it's a marathon. And with the right tools, mindset, and support system by your side, it's a race that you can not only finish but thrive in for years to come. Let's keep running together!

Fine-Tuning Your Financial Plan

As we've navigated the winding path of budgeting and financial management, a recurring theme has emerged: our money journeys are not static, but ever-evolving. Just as our lives shift and change with each passing season, so too must our financial strategies adapt to new circumstances, challenges, and opportunities.

In the preceding sections of this chapter, we've explored the vital importance of regularly reviewing and adjusting our budgets. We began by discussing the power of consistent check-ins—those dedicated moments where we pause to assess our financial progress, celebrate our wins, and identify areas for improvement. Whether conducted weekly, monthly, or quarterly, these regular reviews help us stay accountable, aligned, and agile in our money management.

We then delved into the art of embracing flexibility in our financial plans. Life has a way of throwing us curveballs—unexpected expenses, changes in income, shifting priorities—that can easily derail even the most meticulously crafted budget. By building adaptability into our money mindset, we equip ourselves to navigate these changing tides with grace and resilience. We learn to view our budgets not as rigid rulebooks, but as living, breathing guides that bend and flex with the contours of our lives.

To illustrate these principles in action, we explored real-life examples and success stories of individuals and families who have masterfully navigated the ups and downs of their financial journeys. From the single mother who bounced back from a job loss to the young couple who adjusted their budget to welcome a new baby, these stories remind us that financial success is not about perfection, but about progress, adaptability, and an unwavering commitment to our deepest values and goals.

As we synthesize these key learnings, a few essential tips emerge for fine-tuning our financial plans:

1. Schedule regular financial check-ins and treat them as non-negotiable appointments with ourselves. Whether it's a weekly money date with our partner or a monthly solo review session, creating a consistent rhythm of reflection and adjustment keeps us proactive and empowered in our financial lives.

2. Approach our budgets with a spirit of curiosity and compassion, not judgment or rigidity. When we inevitably encounter challenges or setbacks, we can choose to view them as opportunities for learning and growth, rather than failures or defeats.

3. Cultivate a mindset of flexibility and adaptability, recognizing that change is a natural and necessary part of the financial journey. By holding our plans loosely and staying open to pivots and adjustments, we build the resilience needed to weather any financial storm.

4. Celebrate our wins, both big and small. Whether it's paying off a debt, reaching a savings milestone, or simply staying on track with our budget for a full month, acknowledging our progress fuels our motivation and momentum.

5. Seek out community, support, and inspiration on the journey. Whether it's joining a financial literacy group, working with a trusted advisor, or simply sharing our goals and challenges with loved ones, surrounding ourselves with encouragement and accountability can make all the difference.

As we internalize these lessons and continue fine-tuning our financial strategies, we may find that the process of managing our money transforms from a source of stress and anxiety to one of empowerment and even joy. By approaching our finances with intention, flexibility, and self-compassion, we gradually cultivate a sense of mastery and control over this critical aspect of our lives.

Of course, the journey of financial growth and discovery never truly ends. As we close out this chapter and look ahead to the next, we recognize that there will always be new horizons to explore, new challenges to overcome, and new opportunities to seize. In the concluding sections of this book, we'll delve into strategies for staying the course on our financial journeys for the long haul—

from overcoming plateaus and setbacks to continually expanding our money knowledge and skills. We'll explore how to stay anchored in our values and vision even as the tides of life shift and change, and how to use our financial resources as a powerful tool for crafting a life of purpose, impact, and abundance.

By embracing the principles of consistency, adaptability, and lifelong learning, we equip ourselves to not just survive, but thrive on the ever-unfolding path of financial growth. So let us move forward with curiosity, courage, and a steadfast commitment to the journey—knowing that with each mindful step, we are shaping a future of boundless possibility and promise.

CHAPTER TEN

STAYING THE COURSE, YOUR ROADMAP TO FINANCIAL FREEDOM

Throughout this book, we've explored the transformative power of budgeting—how it can help you take control of your finances, align your spending with your values, and build a strong foundation for your future. But as with any journey, there will be challenges and obstacles along the way. In this final chapter, we'll discuss how to stay the course and maintain your budgeting momentum for the long haul.

We'll start by addressing the inevitable setbacks and plateaus that arise on the path to financial freedom. Whether it's an unexpected expense, a job loss, or a dip in motivation, these bumps in the road can feel discouraging and even derailing. But with the right mindset and strategies, you can not only weather these storms but also emerge stronger and more resilient.

Next, we'll explore the importance of continual learning and growth in your financial journey. Just as your budget will evolve and adapt over time, so too should your financial knowledge and skills. By staying curious, open-minded, and committed to ongoing education, you can unlock new opportunities, navigate changing economic landscapes, and make informed decisions that support your long-term goals.

Finally, we'll discuss the power of celebrating your milestones and reflecting on your progress. In the pursuit of financial freedom, it's easy to become fixated on the end goal and overlook the smaller victories along the way. But by taking the time to acknowledge and savor your achievements—whether it's paying off a debt, reaching a savings target, or making a smart money decision—you can cultivate a sense of momentum, gratitude, and joy that will fuel your motivation for the long run.

As we explore these key themes, we'll offer practical tips, real-life examples, and words of encouragement to help you stay focused, energized, and empowered on your budgeting journey. Because ultimately, financial freedom is about so much more than just numbers on a spreadsheet—it's about creating a life that is abundant, fulfilling, and true to your deepest values and aspirations.

So if you're ready to embrace the adventure ahead, to stay the course even when the path gets rocky, and to unlock the full potential of your financial future—then let's dive in together. Your roadmap to lasting financial freedom starts now.

In the first section, we'll tackle the common setbacks and plateaus that can arise on the budgeting journey, and explore proven strategies for overcoming these challenges with resilience and grace. Get ready to turn obstacles into opportunities and setbacks into stepping stones.

OVERCOMING PLATEAUS AND SETBACKS

Picture this: you've been chugging along on your budgeting journey for a while now, making steady progress towards your financial goals. But then, out of nowhere, life throws you a curveball. Maybe your car breaks down, requiring a costly repair. Maybe your company announces layoffs, and suddenly your job security feels shaky. Or maybe the stock market takes a tumble, and your investments lose a significant chunk of their value.

In moments like these, it's easy to feel discouraged or even defeated. After all, you've been working so hard to stick to your budget and build a stronger financial foundation—why does it suddenly feel like you're back at square one?

First and foremost, it's important to remember that setbacks and plateaus are a normal, inevitable part of any journey—including your financial one. Just like a fitness enthusiast might encounter a weight loss plateau or an injury that sidelines their training, you too will face financial obstacles and challenges along the way. The key is not to let these setbacks derail you completely, but rather to view them as opportunities for growth, learning, and resilience.

So, how can you weather these financial storms and come out stronger on the other side? Let's break it down:

1. **Expect the unexpected:** One of the best ways to prepare for financial setbacks is to, well, expect them. That's why building an emergency fund is such a crucial part of the budgeting process. By setting aside a portion of your income each month into a dedicated savings account, you give yourself a cushion to fall back on when unexpected expenses arise. Aim to build up enough savings to cover at least 3-6 months' worth of essential living expenses, such as rent/mortgage, food, utilities, and transportation.

2. **Adjust your budget:** When a financial setback occurs, it's important to take a step back and reassess your budget. Look for areas where you can temporarily cut back or reallocate funds to address the immediate challenge. For example, if you lose your job, you may need to scale back your discretionary spending (like dining out or subscription services) in order to focus on covering your essential needs. Remember, your budget is a flexible tool that can and should adapt to your changing circumstances.

3. **Communicate and seek support:** Financial stress can feel isolating, but remember that you don't have to face it alone. If you have a partner or family, be open and honest about your situation and work together to create a plan. If you're single, lean on trusted friends or consider joining a support group for people navigating similar financial challenges. Sometimes simply talking through your worries and brainstorming solutions with others can help lighten the emotional load.

4. **Focus on what you can control:** When the stock market is volatile or the economy feels uncertain, it's easy to get caught up in a spiral of anxiety and what-ifs. However, it's important to remember that there are many aspects of your financial life that you can control, even in the face of external challenges. For example, you can control your spending habits, your savings rate, and your debt repayment strategy. By focusing on these controllable factors and letting go of what you can't change, you can maintain a sense of agency and empowerment.

5. **Learn from the experience:** Every financial setback, no matter how painful, offers valuable lessons and insights. As you navigate the challenge, take time to reflect on what you can learn from the experience. What worked well in your response, and what could you improve for next time? How can you build more resilience and adaptability into your financial plan moving forward? By approaching setbacks with a growth mindset, you can transform them from roadblocks into stepping stones.

Ultimately, the path to financial freedom is rarely a straight line. There will be ups and downs, twists and turns, and moments where you feel like you're standing still or even sliding backwards. But by staying committed to your budget, maintaining a flexible and solution-oriented mindset, and leaning on your support system, you can overcome any plateau or setback that comes your way.

Remember, your financial journey is a marathon, not a sprint. It's not about perfection, but rather about progress, resilience, and the willingness to keep putting one foot in front of the other, no matter what obstacles arise.

So the next time you encounter a financial setback, take a deep breath, remind yourself of how far you've already come, and then take the next small step forward. With time, patience, and perseverance, you'll find yourself back on solid ground—and perhaps even stronger and wiser for the experience.

In the next section, we'll explore how continuous learning and education can help you not only overcome financial challenges but also unlock new opportunities for growth and success. By staying curious and committed to your financial development, you can turn setbacks into springboards and plateaus into launchpads. Let's dive in!

CONTINUAL LEARNING AND FINANCIAL GROWTH

Picture your financial journey as a grand adventure, filled with twists, turns, and endless opportunities for discovery. Just like any great explorer, you'll need a trusty map and compass to navigate the terrain ahead. But what if I told you that the most powerful navigation tools are already within your grasp? They're called curiosity and lifelong learning, and they hold the key to unlocking a world of financial growth and possibility.

You see, the landscape of personal finance is always evolving. New technologies emerge, economic conditions shift, and innovative strategies come to light. It's a dynamic, ever-changing world that can feel both exhilarating and overwhelming at times. But here's the good news: by embracing a mindset of continual learning, you can not only keep pace with these changes but also harness them to your advantage.

Think of it like this: when you first started your budgeting journey, you likely had to learn a whole new set of skills and concepts. Maybe you had to wrap your head around the difference between fixed and variable expenses, or learn how to create a realistic savings plan. At first, these ideas might have felt foreign or intimidating. But with time, practice, and a willingness to learn, they gradually became second nature.

The same principle applies as you continue along your financial path. As you encounter new challenges, opportunities, and ideas, your ongoing education will be your guiding light. By staying curious and committed to learning, you'll develop the knowledge, skills, and adaptability you need to thrive in any financial landscape.

So, what does this learning process look like in practice? It can take many forms, depending on your personal preferences and learning style. Some people love curling up with a good book on personal finance, soaking up insights from experts in the field. Others prefer the convenience and immediacy of podcasts, listening to financial wisdom on their daily commute or while doing household chores.

Online courses and workshops can be another fantastic way to deepen your financial knowledge, often in a more structured and interactive format. Many universities, financial institutions, and online learning platforms offer a wide range of classes on topics like investing, retirement planning, and entrepreneurship.

But learning doesn't have to be a solitary pursuit. Attending local meetups, conferences, or discussion groups can be a great way to connect with like-minded individuals and learn from each other's experiences. You might even consider finding a financial mentor or joining a mastermind group to help accelerate your growth and accountability.

As you explore these different learning avenues, there are a few key principles to keep in mind:

1. **Stay open and curious:** Approach each learning opportunity with a beginner's mind, even if you consider yourself financially savvy. Be open to new ideas, perspectives, and approaches, and don't be afraid to ask questions or seek clarification when needed.

2. **Focus on timeless principles:** While it's important to stay attuned to current financial trends and news, don't get too caught up in the latest fads or buzzwords. Instead, focus on building a strong foundation of timeless financial principles, such as budgeting, saving, investing, and risk management.

3. **Apply what you learn:** Knowledge is only powerful if you put it into action. As you gain new financial insights and strategies, look for ways to apply them to your own life and budget. Experiment with different techniques, track your progress, and make adjustments as needed.

4. **Share your knowledge:** As you grow in your financial understanding, consider sharing your insights with others. You might start a blog, lead a workshop, or simply have an honest conversation with a friend or family member who's struggling with their finances. By becoming a teacher and mentor yourself, you'll not only help others along their journey but also deepen your own understanding in the process.

Remember, your financial education is a lifelong journey, not a one-time event. Just as your budget will evolve and adapt over time, so too will your knowledge and skills. By staying curious, committed, and open to new ideas, you'll be well-equipped to navigate whatever financial adventures come your way.

As the old adage goes, "The more you learn, the more you earn." But the rewards of financial education go far beyond your bank balance. By investing in your own learning and growth, you're cultivating a sense of confidence, empowerment, and resilience that will serve you in every area of life.

So keep exploring, keep discovering, and keep growing. Your financial future is bright, and the best is yet to come.

In the final section of this chapter, we'll explore how celebrating milestones and reflecting on your progress can help you stay motivated and energized along your budgeting journey. Get ready to raise a toast to your financial wins, both big and small!

Celebrating Milestones and Looking Ahead

As you've journeyed through the pages of this book, you've explored the ins and outs of budgeting—from crafting your first spending plan to navigating setbacks and embracing lifelong learning. You've discovered that budgeting is so much more than just numbers on a spreadsheet; it's a powerful tool for aligning your money with your values, goals, and dreams.

But here's a truth that's often overlooked in the world of personal finance: the journey is just as important as the destination. It's not just about reaching some far-off financial milestone; it's about the growth, resilience, and self-discovery you experience along the way.

That's why celebrating your progress, both big and small, is such a crucial part of the budgeting process. By taking the time to acknowledge and savor your wins, you're reinforcing the positive habits and mindset shifts that will sustain you for the long haul.

So, what does it look like to celebrate your budgeting milestones? It can be as simple as treating yourself to a favorite meal or activity when you hit a savings goal, or sharing your progress with a trusted friend or accountability partner. The key is to choose rewards that align with your values and bring you genuine joy and satisfaction.

For example, let's say you've been working hard to pay off your credit card debt, and you finally make that last payment. That's a huge accomplishment that deserves to be celebrated! Maybe you treat yourself to a special outing with loved ones, or splurge on a small item you've been saving for. Or perhaps you simply take a moment to close your eyes, take a deep breath, and savor the feeling of freedom and empowerment that comes with being debt-free.

But it's not just the big, flashy milestones that deserve recognition. The smaller, more incremental wins are just as worthy of celebration. Did you stick to your grocery budget this week, even when temptation struck? Did you successfully negotiate a bill or find a creative way to save on a necessary expense? These are the everyday victories that add up over time, and they deserve to be acknowledged and appreciated.

One powerful way to track and celebrate your progress is to keep a financial gratitude journal. Each day or week, take a few minutes to jot down one or two things you're proud of or grateful for in your financial life. It could be a smart money decision you made, a financial lesson you learned, or simply a moment of abundance or generosity that made you smile. Over time, this practice can help you cultivate a deep sense of appreciation and fulfillment, no matter where you are on your budgeting journey.

As you celebrate your milestones and reflect on your progress, it's also important to keep looking ahead with a sense of excitement and possibility. Remember, your budget is a living, breathing document that will evolve and grow with you over time. As your life circumstances change—whether it's a new job, a growing family, or a shifting set of goals and priorities—your budget will be there to support and guide you every step of the way.

The beauty of mastering the fundamentals of budgeting is that it opens up a world of exciting possibilities for your financial future. With a strong foundation in place, you can start dreaming bigger and exploring new horizons. Maybe you'll start investing in the stock market, or saving up for a down payment on your dream home. Maybe you'll launch your own business, or plan a once-in-a-lifetime travel adventure.

Whatever your aspirations may be, your budgeting skills will be the rocket fuel that propels you towards them. By aligning your money with your deepest values and desires, you'll be able to create a life that is rich in every sense of the word—not just financially, but emotionally, relationally, and spiritually as well.

YOUR JOURNEY TO FINANCIAL FREEDOM CONTINUES

As we arrive at the final pages of our exploration into the world of personal finance, it's worth pausing to reflect on how far we've come. Throughout these chapters, we've delved deep into the transformative power of budgeting—not merely as a mechanical process of tracking numbers, but as a tool for aligning our money with our deepest values, goals, and dreams.

We began our journey by laying the essential foundations of financial success: crafting a budget that accurately reflects our income, expenses, and priorities; building an emergency fund to weather life's inevitable storms; and developing strategies for paying down debt and staying motivated on the path to financial freedom.

As we progressed, we discovered that true financial wellbeing extends beyond the confines of spreadsheets and bank balances. We explored the art of intentional living—of using our money as a tool to create a life rich in purpose, joy, and generosity. We learned to distinguish between needs and wants, to find contentment in simplicity, and to invest in experiences and relationships that bring us lasting fulfillment.

We then ventured into the realm of investing, demystifying the often-intimidating world of stocks, bonds, and portfolios. We discovered that successful investing is less about chasing hot stock tips or timing the market, and more about harnessing the power of consistency, patience, and long-term thinking. By starting early, diversifying our portfolios, and keeping our costs low, we learned that anyone can build wealth steadily over time.

But perhaps the most powerful lesson threaded throughout these pages is that our financial journeys are never static, but always evolving. As we've seen, life has a way of presenting us with unexpected twists and turns—job losses and windfalls, baby announcements and medical emergencies, shifts in our goals and values. The key to navigating these changing tides lies not in rigidly clinging to a single plan, but in cultivating a mindset of adaptability, resilience, and lifelong learning.

By regularly reviewing our budgets, celebrating our wins, and course-correcting when necessary, we develop the financial agility to ride out any storm. By surrounding ourselves with knowledge, support, and inspiration—whether through books, workshops, or trusted mentors—we equip ourselves to seize new opportunities and rise to new challenges. And by staying connected to our deepest reasons for pursuing financial freedom in the first place—our cherished relationships, our heartfelt passions, our visions for a better world—we infuse our money management with a profound sense of meaning and purpose.

As we close this chapter of our financial education, let us remember that the journey towards lasting prosperity is not a sprint, but a marathon—one that extends far beyond these pages. The skills, habits, and mindsets we've cultivated here will serve as our compass and roadmap as we navigate the winding paths ahead.

When we encounter obstacles and setbacks, as we inevitably will, we can draw on our arsenal of proven strategies and unwavering self-belief to overcome them. When we find ourselves in seasons of abundance and opportunity, we can lean into our values and channel our resources towards the people, causes, and dreams that set our souls on fire. And through it all, we can find strength and inspiration in the knowledge that with each intentional step, each mindful choice, we are shaping a future of boundless possibility.

So as you close this book and embark on the next leg of your financial adventure, know that you carry within you all the tools and wisdom you need to craft a life of true prosperity. A life where money is not the end goal, but a powerful means to express your deepest values, to uplift your loved ones and communities, and to leave a legacy of positive impact on the world.

Your journey to financial freedom is not ending here; it is only just beginning. And with your newfound knowledge, your ever-expanding skills, and your unshakeable commitment to the path of growth, there is no limit to the abundance, joy, and fulfillment that awaits you.

May you always remember the immense power that lies within your choices, your habits, and your dreams. May you have the courage to continually stretch beyond your comfort zone, to embrace the unknown with an open and curious heart. And may you forever trust in your inherent worthiness, your boundless resilience, and your extraordinary capacity to shape a life of profound meaning and purpose.

Thank you for joining me on this journey of financial discovery and transformation. Here's to your next chapter—and to a lifetime of ever-deepening prosperity, abundance, and joy.

The key learning points from this final chapter include:

1. Financial freedom is a lifelong journey of growth, adaptability, and learning. By staying committed to the process and continually refining our strategies, we can navigate any challenge that comes our way.

2. True prosperity goes beyond numbers—it's about using our money to craft a life aligned with our deepest values and purpose. As we grow in our financial skills, we gain the power to uplift ourselves, our loved ones, and our world in profound ways.

3. Building wealth is a marathon, not a sprint. By cultivating patience, consistency, and a long-term perspective, we can harness the power of compound growth and steadily build financial abundance over time.

4. Obstacles and setbacks are inevitable parts of the journey. By reframing them as opportunities for learning and growth, and by drawing on our inner resilience and proven strategies, we can overcome any financial challenge.

5. Surrounding ourselves with knowledge, support, and inspiration is crucial for sustained financial growth. By continually expanding our money skills and mindsets, and by plugging into uplifting communities, we equip ourselves to thrive in any environment.

6. Ultimate financial success lies in aligning our money with our deepest values and reasons for being. When we use our resources to live and give from a place of profound meaning and purpose, we experience a level of wealth that goes far beyond material riches.

As you integrate these final insights and reflect on all you've learned throughout this transformative journey, know that you already hold within you the keys to lasting financial freedom. Your path forward from here will be uniquely your own—shaped by your particular dreams, challenges, and triumphs. But armed with the timeless principles and practical wisdom you've gained, you now have a robust roadmap to guide your way.

Wherever your financial adventures take you next, may you always lead with your deepest values, always trust in your innate resilience and potential, and always remember the immense power you hold to craft a life of extraordinary abundance, impact, and joy. Here's to your next bold steps on the path of lifelong financial growth and fulfillment.

As we close out this remarkable journey together, I invite you to pause and honor just how far you've come. From those first tentative steps into the world of budgeting and money management to the profound shifts you've made in your financial habits and mindsets—you've blossomed into an empowered, purposeful steward of your resources and your dreams.

So before you turn the page on this chapter of your story, take a moment to celebrate all that you've learned, all that you've overcome, and all that you've become. Reflect on the seeds of knowledge you've planted, the new shoots of abundance that are already blooming in your life. And lean into the unshakable knowing that this is just the beginning.

Printed in Great Britain
by Amazon